L ANGUAGE ARTS
SKILLS & STRATEGIES

LEVEL 7

L ANGUAGE ARTS
SKILLS & STRATEGIES

LEVEL **3**
LEVEL **4**
LEVEL **5**
LEVEL **6**
LEVEL **7** ⇦
LEVEL **8**

Production: Pearl Production
Cover Design: I.Q. Design, Inc.

SADDLEBACK
PUBLISHING·INC.
Three Watson
Irvine, CA 92618-2767
Website: www.sdlback.com

ISBN 1-56254-841-7

Printed in the United States of America
10 09 08 07 06 05 9 8 7 6 5 4 3 2 1

CONTENTS

CONTENTS

Welcome to
LANGUAGE ARTS SKILLS & STRATEGIES

Saddleback Publishing is proud to introduce this important supplement to your basal language arts curriculum. Our goal in creating this series is two-fold: to help on-level and below-level students improve their writing skills by defining and practicing discrete skills, and to provide you, the teacher, with maximum flexibility in deciding when and how to assign these exercises.

All lessons are reproducible. That makes them ideal for homework, extra credit assignments, cooperative learning groups, or focused drill practice for selected ELL or remedial students. A quick scan of the book's Table of Contents will enable you to individualize instruction according to the varied needs of your students.

Correlated to the latest research and current language arts standards in most states, the instructional design of *Language Arts Skills & Strategies* is unusually comprehensive for a supplementary program. All grade-appropriate grammar, mechanics, and usage skills are thoroughly presented from the ground up.

Assessment and evaluation of student understanding and ability is an ongoing process. A variety of methods and strategies should be used to ensure that the student is being assessed and evaluated in a fair and comprehensive manner. Here again, reproducible lessons are ideal in that they can be used for both pre- and post-testing. Always keep in mind that the assessment should take into consideration the opportunities the student had to learn the information and practice the skills presented. The strategies for assessment are left for you to determine and are dependent on your students and your particular instructional plan. The Table of Contents lists the activity by skill and can be used to assist you as you develop your assessment plan.

A capital letter at the beginning of a word is a signal to readers that the word is important in some way. Capitalize the names of streets, cities, states, countries, and continents. Also capitalize the names of buildings, parks, mountains, and bodies of water.

Asia   Canada   Arkansas   Polk County   Seattle   Lake Tahoe   Appalachian Mountains

Directions: Read the following paragraph about Sandhill Cranes. Underline the words that should be capitalized.

Six-million-year-old fossils prove that sandhill cranes are the oldest still-living species of birds. Sandhill cranes are native to wisconsin, much of north america, and eastern russia. Three types of sandhill cranes, the greater, the lesser, and the canadian, are migratory. Most of the migratory types spend their summers along a broad "belt" that stretches from ontario and michigan to british columbia and alaska to eastern siberia. Smaller populations of migratory sandhills pass the summers in western pennsylvania, eastern ohio, northern california, south central oregon, southern idaho, and northern utah. The states of florida, texas, new mexico, arizona, and california and the country of mexico host the birds for the winter. Lesser sandhill cranes have the longest migratory route of any crane: 14,000 miles round trip!

Directions: Imagine that a new continent has suddenly arisen out of the Earth's oceans. Create a name for the continent as well as for the other geographical locations featured in the travel ad below. Be sure to capitalize all geographical locations.

Tour the Earth's Newest Continent!

Travel to the continent of _____, which has recently arisen out of the _____ Ocean! Visit _____, its largest country. Travel through its most picturesque state, _____. Stay a day or two in the beautiful city of _____. Spend some time in the quaint village of _____, nestled high in the _____ Mountains. While you're there, climb Mount _____, where the mouth of the _____ River is located. From _____ Peak, see the beautiful counties of _____ and _____ stretched out below. Swim in Lake _____ and experience the breathtaking _____ Falls. See this exciting new land today!

Name: _____   **Date:** _____

The names of many events and periods of time are capitalized.

the Roaring 20s   World War I

Directions: The letters of each of the following events and periods of time have been scrambled. Rearrange the letters to form the name and write it on the line, being sure to capitalize correctly. Read the clues for help.

1. lvici arw _____ (blue versus gray)

2. zajz gea _____ (hot times for music)

3. rhecfn elonotviru _____ (Marie Antoinette lost her head)

4. sacurjsi iredop _____ (age of the giants)

5. ycmsiolp _____ (ancient games)

6. lgdo shur _____ (strike it rich in California)

7. dimdel esag _____ (time of castles and knights)

8. cynkkeut rybed _____ (a horse race)

9. soonbt eta rypta _____ (protesting the King's taxes)

10. nceareisans _____ (cultural "rebirth" of the 15th and 16th century)

11. trialdsuin vureotioln _____ (the age of machinery)

12. snichee wen reya _____ (parades with dragons)

13. drami agsr _____ (New Orleans's big day)

14. heart yda _____ (celebrating the planet)

15. prues olbw _____ (a day for armchair quarterbacks)

Capitalize the names of documents, religions, businesses, organizations, schools, and teams.

the Declaration of Independence   League of Women Voters

The names of nationalities and languages should be capitalized as well.

Spanish   Turkish   Dutch

Directions: These sentences are missing some capital letters. Rewrite the words that should be capitalized correctly on the lines.

1. In cartoons, republicans are often represented by an elephant, and a donkey stands for democrats.

_____

2. Tim bought a spanish/english dictionary at capital books.

_____

3. The United States constitution outlines the rights of citizens.

_____

4. Lincoln junior high's basketball team, the leopards, has won three games so far.

_____

5. The springdale soccer association has 227 members.

_____

6. Martin Luther was a german who founded the lutheran church.

_____

7. Greg's dad used to belong to greenpeace.

_____

8. The magna carta is the most famous document in british history.

_____

9. The southside chess club meets at the java hut.

_____

10. If you are swiss, you probably speak french, italian, or german.

_____

Name: _____   Date: _____

It is easy to remember the rules of capitalization for some titles, because they are almost always used before a name: Mr. Harper, Ms. Lee. You probably don't even think about the rule anymore because if you didn't capitalize these titles, it would look odd to you: mr. Harper, ms. Lee. But other titles, such as "coach" and "senator," can easily be used without a name. Follow this rule: if a title is used as a name or as part of a person's name, capitalize it.

The **coach** told us to run laps.

We talked to **Coach Hasselhof**. I asked **Coach** about practice next week.

One of our state **senators** came to the meeting.

We voted for **Senator Murphy**. Excuse me, **Senator**, may I ask you a question?

Put a period after titles that are abbreviated.

Mrs. Vindu   Gov. Kerr

Directions: Read each sentence. If the sentence contains no capitalization errors, write OK on the line. If it contains an error, write the word or words correctly on the line.

1. Who is the class president? _____

The secretary will arrive before president Tomlinson. _____

2. What did dad say about the broken window? _____

Jason's dad will come pick us up at 5:00. _____

3. Sam might become a general in the army. _____

Will General Noonan make a statement? _____

4. Tim has an appointment with doctor Wilson this afternoon. _____

All the Doctors read the research report. _____

5. How many Aunts do you have? _____

A letter from Aunt Marietta arrived today. _____

BONUS: Write two sentences for the title below. In the first sentence, use the title as a name or as part of a name. In the second sentence, use the title alone. Be sure to capitalize correctly.

captain

_____

_____

When writing the title of a book, magazine, newspaper, movie, play, or TV show, capitalize the first and last words, all important words in between, and all verbs, no matter how short. Do not capitalize the word *to*, articles, prepositions, or coordinating conjunctions unless they are the first or last word of the title.

In print, titles are in italics. When you write, underline titles.

Have you read <u>The Wrong Side of the Coin</u>?

Some titles use quotation marks instead of underlining. Set quotation marks around the titles of songs, short stories, poems, articles, and book chapters. Capitalize them just as you would the title of a book.

Book: *Walk Two Roads* **Magazine Article:** "Mountain Biking: How Safe Is It?"
TV Show: *The Simpsons* **Short Story:** "The Song of the Whales"
Movie: *Night of the Lizards* **Poem:** "A Simple Wish"

Directions: Capitalize the following titles according to the guidelines above. Underline or use quotation marks as needed.

1. Book title: the rise and fall of the roman empire _____

_____

2. Poem title: one shoe, two feet _____

3. Song title: it's easy to remember _____

4. Magazine article title: hurricane isabel slams the coast _____

_____

5. Story title: the princess and the pea _____

6. Movie title: miracle on 34th street _____

7. Newspaper name: the chicago daily register _____

8. Play title: romeo and juliet _____

9. Newspaper article title: couple marries 52 years later _____

_____

10. TV show name: malcolm in the middle _____

BONUS: Complete each sentence with a title. Use capitalization, underlining, and quotation marks correctly.

One of my favorite songs is _____.

On TV, I often watch _____.

Name: _____ **Date:** _____

When you write a letter to someone you know well, you are writing a friendly letter. The greeting of a letter should be capitalized. In the body of the letter, the first letter of every sentence should be capitalized. Capitalize the first word and any proper names in the closing of the letter.

You may choose to add a P. S. to your letter as well. P. S. stands for "post" (after) and "script" (writing). Capitalize both letters of this abbreviation and follow each with a period.

Directions: The letter below is not capitalized correctly. Correct the capitalization errors by crossing out each error and writing the correction above it.

1312 union st.

scottsdale, az 55555

august 25, 2006

dear sam,

i'm so proud of you for winning the talent show contest. i'll bet you impressed them all with your saxophone playing. your mother says you are getting very good and that you're actually practicing on a regular basis! good for you!

how is molly doing? is she planning on going out for basketball again this year? and how about you? will you be going out for any sports now that you're in middle school? also, are you planning on joining band? i certainly hope so! with the talent show out of the way, you're probably getting ready for the new school year. here's hoping you have a very successful one!

warmest regards,

aunt rita

ps

keep up the practicing. it sounds like it's paying off!

Name: _____   Date: _____

Language Arts Skills & Strategies, Level 7 • Saddleback Publishing, Inc. ©2005 • 3 Watson, Irvine, CA 92618 • Phone (888) 735-2225 • www.sdlback.com   11

An abbreviation is a shortened form of a word. Most, but not all, abbreviations end with a period.

TITLES	TIME AND DATES
Dr. (Doctor)	a.m. or A.M. (ante meridiem)
Jr. (Junior)	p.m. or P.M. (post meridiem)
Sgt. (Sergeant)	Mon. (Monday)
R.N. (Registered Nurse)	Dec. (December)
	min. (minute)

BUSINESSES	UNITS OF MEASUREMENT
Co. (Company)	in. (inch)
Inc. (Incorporated)	yd (yard)
Corp. (Corporation)	kg (kilogram)
Ltd. (Limited)	hp (horsepower)

PHRASES	ADDRESSES
ASAP (as soon as possible)	IL (Illinois)
MIA (missing in action)	Ave. (Avenue)

ORGANIZATIONS	COMMON LATIN PHRASES
NASA (National Aeronautics and Space Administration)	etc. (et cetera: and so on)
NPR (National Public Radio)	e.g. (exempli gratia: for example)

Directions: Write the abbreviation for each word or phrase. Use a dictionary if you need help.

1. Limited _____
2. National Public Radio _____
3. centimeter _____
4. California _____
5. National Hockey League _____
6. revolutions per minute _____
7. Captain _____
8. National Broadcasting Corporation _____
9. People for the Ethical Treatment of Animals _____
10. gallon _____

Directions: Write the word or words these abbreviations stand for. Use a dictionary if you need help.

11. Sr. _____
12. mph _____
13. min. _____
14. AZ _____
15. rt. _____
16. NYPD _____
17. Co. _____
18. K.O. _____
19. oz. _____
20. CO _____

Name: _____ Date: _____

Directions: Write the abbreviation from the box that goes with each item.

Pkwy.	BBC	Fri.	CD	IRA	MN	NOW	NCAA
MO	NASA	USO	NC	CEO	VIP	ft	CBS	USC
WW II	CPA	hp	Aug.	UNICEF	CIA		

1. National Organization for Women _____

2. Columbia Broadcasting System _____

3. compact disc _____

4. North Carolina _____

5. Certified Public Accountant _____

6. National Aeronautics and Space Administration _____

7. National Collegiate Athletic Association _____

8. University of Southern California _____

9. Parkway _____

10. Second World War _____

11. Minnesota _____

12. Missouri _____

13. Central Intelligence Agency _____

14. individual retirement account _____

15. August _____

16. Friday _____

17. United Nations Children's Fund _____

18. very important person _____

19. United Service Organizations _____

20. horsepower _____

21. British Broadcasting Corporation _____

22. Chief Executive Officer _____

23. foot _____

Name: _____ **Date:** _____

Directions: These sentences are missing some capital letters. Rewrite them correctly on the lines.

1. My french teacher, mrs. dubonnet, has lived in the united states for eleven years.

   _____

2. This article, "how to jumpstart your exercise routine," was written by dr. lynnette richards.

   _____

3. Is fenway park in boston or new york?

   _____

4. the concert on independence day will feature the carterville children's chorus singing such songs as "america the beautiful."

   _____

5. Parker met up with his cousins and uncle stan at the his favorite restaurant, the barbecue shack.

   _____

Directions: The letter below is not capitalized correctly. Correct the capitalization errors by crossing out each error and writing the correction above it. Then write the abbreviations for the underlined words and phrases on the lines below.

46 hillcrest <u>drive</u>

frankfurt, <u>illinois</u> 55555

<u>december</u> 18, 2005

dear grandpa,

have you heard the news? david is going to be named <u>chief executive officer</u> of his company! They announced it yesterday on the local <u>public broadcasting service</u> station. David junior is so proud of his daddy. so are we!

with love,

molly

_____ _____ _____ _____ _____

Name: _____ **Date:** _____

Every sentence must have an end mark. End marks are signals. They tell readers that they have reached the end of an idea. End marks also tell readers how to read sentences.

- **Periods** close statements or commands: *Curling became an Olympic sport in 1998.*

When an abbreviation falls at the end of a statement or command, an additional period is not necessary: *The Olympic curling team met every morning at 6:30 A.M.*

- **Question marks** close sentences that ask direct questions: *How did curling get its name?*
- **Exclamation points** close sentences that show surprise or strong emotion: *Wow! The women's curling team from Scotland won a gold medal!*

Directions: Supply end marks for each sentence in the following passage.

Mention the sport of curling, and most people scratch their heads and ask, "Is that a sport___" Curling, which is played on ice, originated in Scotland in the 16th century___ Equipment for the game includes brooms—yes, brooms and granite rocks___ The rocks weigh a whopping 42 pounds___ A curling tournament consists of 10 "ends," similar to baseball's innings___ Why is the sport called curling___ The rocks tend to curve, or "curl," as they slide towards the target___

A curling team consists of four players___ During an "end" each player will slide two rocks towards a target___ The target is a twelve-foot circle 130 feet away___ After all the rocks have been thrown, the score is tallied up___ One point is awarded for each rock that is closest to the center of the target___

Where do the brooms come in___ Oddly enough, the brooms are used not to push the rocks, but to sweep the ice in front of them as they glide toward the target___ The idea is to create enough friction on the ice to form a thin layer of moisture between the ice and the rock___ Amazingly, this simple trick can help the rock slide an additional 15 feet___

Approximately 15,000 curlers live in the United States, with the majority being from Wisconsin and Minnesota___ Canada has almost 1.2 million of the estimated 1.5 million curlers in the world___ That's a lot of curlers___

Name: _____   **Date:** _____

Directions: Write four sentences that someone might say in the following situations. Write a declarative sentence, an exclamatory sentence, an interrogatory sentence, and an imperative sentence.

EXAMPLE
Situation: Your dog is chasing a cat down the street.
Declarative: I should have locked the gate.
Exclamatory: That cat is fast!
Interrogatory: Where is that cat going?
Imperative: Go get Bowser's leash.

1. *Situation:* A teacher is announcing a class trip to an amusement park.

   Declarative: _____

   Exclamatory: _____

   Interrogatory: _____

   Imperative: _____

2. *Situation:* Two canoeists are approaching a waterfall.

   Declarative: _____

   Exclamatory: _____

   Interrogatory: _____

   Imperative: _____

3. *Situation:* A group of friends are planning a party for another friend.

   Declarative: _____

   Exclamatory: _____

   Interrogatory: _____

   Imperative: _____

4. *Situation:* The members of a new rock band are practicing together for the first time.

   Declarative: _____

   Exclamatory: _____

   Interrogatory: _____

   Imperative: _____

Name: _____ **Date:** _____

Possessive nouns show that someone or something has or owns something. Follow these rules to form possessive nouns.

singular nouns.	add –s	**Tessa's** piano lessons are on Tuesdays.
plural nouns ending in –s	add –'	Those two **students'** essays tied for first place.
plural nouns not ending in –s	add –s	Professor Bingham teaches a class on **women's** rights.

Directions: Complete each sentence by writing the possessive form of the noun in parentheses on the line.

1. (elephant) The preschoolers were allowed to touch the _____ trunk.

2. (Mr. Sahu) _____ creative writing club meets on Wednesdays.

3. (everyone) The photographer took _____ pictures.

4. (Evans) Two raccoons invaded the _____ garden.

5. (people) Elena Sanchez was the _____ choice for mayor.

6. (Somebody) _____ dog is in our yard.

7. (deer) The _____ habitat was destroyed by a housing development.

8. (committee) The _____ duties were made clear at the meeting.

9. (politicians) The _____ viewpoints were very different.

10. (herd) Authorities could not locate the _____ owner.

Directions: Decide whether each underlined word is punctuated correctly. Correct any mistakes on the lines provided. If there are no mistakes, write *Correct as is.*

11. The <u>teachers</u> aide picked up the <u>childrens'</u> toys at the end of the day.

   _____

12. The courtroom waited for the <u>jurys'</u> decision.

   _____

13. Our <u>club's</u> mission is to find homes for stray animals.

   _____

14. <u>Brianna's</u> bike was stolen.

   _____

15. The <u>actors'</u> dressing rooms were recently redecorated.

   _____

In the contractions *it's*, *he's*, and *she's*, *–'s* can stand for *is* or *has*. The *–'d* in contractions such as *I'd* and *they'd* can stand for *had* or *would*.

When you contract something, you shorten it. Contractions draw words together and shorten them into one word. Contractions are formed by leaving out certain letters and replacing them with an apostrophe.

VERB + NOT	PRONOUN + VERB	HELPING VERB + HAVE
has not–hasn't	he had–he'd	should have–should've
is not–isn't	they will–they'll	must have–must've
could not–couldn't	it is–it's	could have–could've
will not–won't	she would–she'd	would have–would've

Directions: Read the following paragraph and cross out any pairs of words that can be made into contractions. Write the contraction in the space above. You should have ten contractions when you have finished.

Walking sticks are odd little creatures. Their scientific name, phasmida, comes from the Greek word *phasma*, meaning "ghost." Walking sticks were not ever considered to be real ghosts. The name simply reflects their ability to seemingly disappear by blending into their surroundings. Many walking sticks are a dull gray, green, or brown. They cannot be easily spotted against a background of twigs and leaves. If they are disturbed, they will lay motionless for hours, actually pretending to be a stick. Sometimes they will even sway from side to side in an attempt to mimic a twig that is blowing in the wind. If they sense real danger, some walking sticks emit a foul-smelling substance that drives intruders away. One species even has a defensive spray that will cause temporary blindness. But perhaps the oddest thing about them is that if a female walking stick cannot find a mate, she is capable of reproducing without one! Now that is weird—and a little scary!

Name: _____ **Date:** _____

A series is a list of three or more items. The items might be words, phrases, or clauses. Use commas to separate items in a series. Use the word *and* or *or* before the last item in the series.

Terrence washed, peeled, and sliced the cucumber.

You'll find the ingredients in the refrigerator, on the shelf, and in that bowl.

Leaving a comma out can change the meaning of a sentence.

Incorrect: *The people I admire most are my parents, Abraham Lincoln and Amelia Earhart.*

Are this writer's parents really Abraham Lincoln and Amelia Earhart? Probably not.

Correct: *The people I admire most are my parents, Abraham Lincoln, and Amelia Earhart.*

Directions: Rewrite each sentence, adding commas where needed.

1. The plane tickets my money and my passport are in this bag.

_____

2. Mr. Davidson showed Frankie Vic and I how to fix a flat.

_____

3. The ball rolled off the table across the floor and out the door.

_____

4. Would you like to play a game watch a movie or go for a walk?

_____

5. My bulletin board is covered with photos of my friends Lance Armstrong and Prince William.

_____

6. Red blue purple and teal are the colors Quentin chose for his poster.

_____

7. Brush your teeth after breakfast after lunch and before you go to bed.

_____

8. Wear sunscreen a wide-brimmed hat and sunglasses at the beach.

_____

9. This recipe calls for a pint of cream half a cup of sugar and two cups of sliced strawberries.

_____

10. The pink slippers are decorated with sequins ribbon and silk flowers.

_____

Use a comma and a coordinating conjunction to join two sentences.

COORDINATING CONJUNCTION	MEANING	EXAMPLE
for	because	Rise and shine, **for** the sun is up.
and	in addition	Brent makes the toast, **and** his little brother eats it.
but	however	The movie was good, **but** it was too long.
or	shows a choice	We might stay here, **or** we might go out.
yet	even though	David is tired, **yet** he's still awake.
so	as a result	It started raining hard, **so** I shut the windows.

Directions: Combine each pair of sentences to form a compound sentence. Use a comma and the coordinating conjunction in parentheses.

1. Sometimes Rory stays up late. He's always tired in the morning. (but)

_____

2. The procession of marchers carried candles. The night was dark. (for)

_____

3. The computer is acting strangely. Let's take it to the repair shop. (so)

_____

4. Tracy tried on the red jeans. They were too short for her. (but)

_____

5. Many people are afraid of spiders. Most are harmless. (yet)

_____

6. Use heavy tape to attach the sign to the pole. It will fall off. (or)

_____

7. Lionel ran as fast as he could. He missed the bus. (but)

_____

8. Sheri called me last night at 8:00. I didn't get off the phone until 9:00! (and)

_____

9. Millie claims she wants to get more exercise. She always protests when I suggest we take the stairs instead of the elevator. (yet)

_____

10. That band's last CD was terrible. This new one isn't any better. (and)

_____

Name: _____ Date: _____

An interrupter is a word or phrase that interrupts a sentence, such as *as a matter of fact* and *unfortunately.* It may appear at the beginning, in the middle, or at the end of a sentence. Use commas to set off an interrupter.

> **In my opinion,** Quatro's has the best pizza in town. Krusti's, **on the other hand,** has terrible pizza. Quatro's is expensive, **unfortunately**.

COMMON INTERRUPTERS

unfortunately	by the way	as a result	in addition	I believe
luckily	for example	however	of course	as a matter of fact

Use commas to set off the name of someone who is being spoken to directly.

> Melanie, will you give me a call when you get home?
> Will you, Melanie, give me a call when you get home?
> Will you give me a call when you get home, Melanie?

Directions: Insert commas where they are needed.

1. The picnic starts at 2:00 this afternoon Lindsey.

2. Unfortunately it looks like it might rain.

3. The weather report in fact says there is a 75% chance of a storm.

4. The report could be wrong about that of course.

5. However they are usually correct about things like that.

Directions: Rewrite each sentence, adding an interrupter or a person's name.

6. A little rain won't ruin our picnic.

   _____

7. We can take our raincoats and umbrellas.

   _____

8. My umbrella is big enough to share.

   _____

9. The picnic tables are under a shelter.

   _____

10. We'll stay perfectly dry.

   _____

Name: _____   **Date:** _____

An appositive is a word or phrase that defines or explains a noun in a sentence. Appositives must follow the noun they define and must be set off with commas.

Kelly, a basketball player, has size 12 feet.
Kelly buys his shoes at Monson's, a shoe store downtown.

Directions: Find the appositive in each sentence. Add commas where needed.

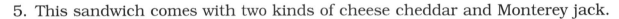

1. Lianna my best friend moved away last year.

2. Carmen and Jeremy joined Rock the Vote an organization of young voters.

3. Parker is taking lessons on the vibraphone an instrument related to the xylophone.

4. The ring was set with a large cubic zirconia an artificial diamond.

5. This sandwich comes with two kinds of cheese cheddar and Monterey jack.

6. Today in art class we learned about Camille Claudel a French sculptress.

7. Marcus's car a convertible is black with red flames painted on it.

8. It is easy to grow arugula a salad green with a peppery bite.

9. Today's special a club sandwich comes with a cup of soup and a small salad.

10. Rachel asked Miss Chen her favorite babysitter to play a game with her.

Directions: Rewrite each sentence, adding an appositive.

11. Jason and Sam went to lunch at Sandy's Subs.

_____

12. Sam ordered the Big Kahuna.

_____

13. Jason could eat only half of his Heavy Hitter.

_____

14. Later, the boys walked down West Avenue to the science museum.

_____

15. Mr. Fallon had suggested they see the new exhibit.

_____

Name: _____   **Date:** _____

Interjections are words that show emotion. An interjections that shows a strong feeling may stand alone and end with an exclamation point. An interjection that shows a milder feeling may appear at the beginning of a sentence, followed by a comma.

Hey! My notebook is missing! Oh, it's here in my backpack.

COMMON INTERJECTIONS

Hurray	Aha	Brr	Whew
Good grief	Oh	Grr	Wow
Hey	Oh, no	Oops	Ugh
Ah	Uh-oh	Ouch	Yuck

Introductory words such as *yes, no,* and *well* are often used at the beginning of a sentence. They should be followed by a comma.

Yes, I would like to go to the movie with you.

Well, what time does it start?

Directions: Add the correct punctuation after each interjection or introductory word.

1. Oh___ what a beautiful night for taking a stroll.

2. Ouch___ I got a paper cut from that magazine.

3. Aha___ We've finally discovered the solution to our problem.

4. Oh, no___ I spilled my drink on my art project, and now it's ruined!

5. Hey___ what's the name of that band you like so much?

Directions: Complete each sentence by adding an appropriate interjection or introductory word and punctuation.

6. _____ I've never seen such a big truck!

7. _____ It's absolutely freezing in here.

8. _____ Justin forgot to take his lunch again.

9. _____ it feels so good when you scratch my back.

10. _____ I'm so mad at this computer!

11. _____ It's snowing!

12. _____ I don't feel like raking the yard right now.

13. _____ I'm so relieved that I found my lost keys.

14. _____ something smells funny in here.

15. _____ I have discovered a clue to the mystery!

Name: _____   **Date:** _____

When you write a speaker's exact words, you are writing a direct quotation. Begin a direct quotation with a capital letter. If it comes at the end of a sentence, introduce it with a comma. Put the end mark inside the last quotation marks.

DeShaun asked, "What was that strange sound?"

The rules are different when a direct quotation comes at the beginning of a sentence. If the quotation is an exclamation or a question, put the end mark inside the quotation marks. If it is a statement or a command, use a comma instead.

Statement: "It sounded like somebody snoring," said Cody.
Command: "Make sure the door is locked," ordered Sam.
Question: "Isn't that your dog, DeShaun?" Tessa asked.
Exclamation: "What a bunch of sillies we are!" Jennifer exclaimed.

Directions: Each sentence contains a direct quotation. Rewrite each sentence, adding commas, capital letters, and quotation marks.

1. Who left their shoes on the stairs Toya asked.

2. Jennifer answered it wasn't me!

3. Maybe it was John Michael said.

4. He never puts anything away Jennifer exclaimed.

5. Yeah, and he left his bike in the driveway yesterday continued Michael.

6. What a lazybones exclaimed Jennifer.

7. Michael observed these shoes are pink and red.

8. Toya asked does John wear pink shoes?

9. I seriously doubt it replied Michael.

10. Oh, they're mine Jennifer said sheepishly.

Name: _____ Date: _____

Sometimes a direct quotation is divided in two parts. Each part should be in quotation marks. If the second part of the quotation is part of the same sentence, begin it with a small letter. Set a comma after the word that comes directly before the second part.

"Well, well," said Hannah, "look who finally decided to show up."

If the second part of the quotation starts a new sentence, begin it with a capital letter.

"I'm so sorry I'm late," said Amy, blushing. "Have you been waiting long?"

Directions: Rewrite the groups of words as one or two sentences with direct quotations, adding commas, periods, question marks, capital letters, and quotation marks where needed.

1. For your information Hannah replied about an hour. (one sentence)

   _____

2. I'm sorry Amy said are you mad at me? (two sentences)

   _____

3. How would you feel Hannah snapped if I made you wait that long? (one sentence)

   _____

4. It really shows a lack of respect continued Hannah are my feelings not important to you? (two sentences)

   _____

5. You're right, Hannah said Amy how can I make it up to you? (two sentences)

   _____

Directions: Continue the dialogue between Hannah and Amy. Punctuate according to the above guidelines.

_____

_____

_____

_____

_____

_____

_____

Name: _____ **Date:** _____

In some cases, a colon can be used to introduce a list. Use a colon after phrases such as *the following, the following things, these,* and *these things* when they introduce a list. The list may consist of one or more items. The items may be nouns, adjectives, phrases, or clauses.

In the last 20 years, technology has brought consumers <u>many new products</u>: VCR's, desktop computers, and video games, to name a few.

Use a colon ONLY after a clause that can stand on its own as a sentence.

Incorrect: In the last 20 years, technology has brought consumers: VCR's, desktop computers, and video games, to name a few.

Directions: Insert a colon between the list of items and the word or words that introduce the list in each sentence.

EXAMPLE: This shirt is available in four colors: red, blue, purple, and brown.

1. I have three favorite books The Borrowers, My Side of the Mountain, and Old Yeller.

2. This report covers two subjects the music of India and Indian folk dances.

3. This movie has it all a love story, a car chase, and a happy ending.

4. After being a camp counselor for three summers in a row, Kiki made an important decision she would study child psychology in college.

5. On the first day of school, students are expected to have the following supplies three notebooks, pens and pencils, and a three-ring binder.

6. "In my opinion," Chad said, "the only game worth playing is this chess."

7. Before Lana left for Brazil, she bought several articles of clothing a lightweight jacket, hiking shoes, and cargo pants.

8. When choosing a pet, it is important to keep in mind the following the size of your home and how much time you will have to play with the pet.

9. The note from the office read, "The following students should report to Mrs. McRoberts Robert Johnson, Treena Horn, Eric Shea, and Carla Barnes."

10. The teacher advised Lynell to pay more attention to these problem areas punctuation and paragraphing.

BONUS: Write a sentence to introduce this list.

low, medium, and high

_____

Name: _____ **Date:** _____

You have learned that two closely related sentences can be joined with a comma and a coordinating conjunction such as *and, or,* or *but.* You can often use a semicolon (;) in place of the comma and coordinating conjunction.

With a Coordinating Conjunction: Kelsey is a good student, **and** she always has her assignments done.

With a Semicolon: Kelsey is a good student**;** she always has her assignments done.

Remember, the idea on each side of the semicolon must be able to stand on its own as a complete sentence, or independent clause.

Incorrect: *I've decided not to go to the game; since I'm coming down with a cold.* *("Since I'm coming down with a cold" cannot stand alone as a sentence.)*

Correct: *I've decided not to go to the game; I'm coming down with a cold.*

Directions: Use an independent clause from the box to complete each sentence. Make sure the ideas in both parts of the completed sentence are closely related.

> he runs on his wheel and climbs up a tiny ladder
> she prefers to be left alone most of the time
> Slinky would just love to eat him
> she crawled under the sofa and hasn't been seen since
> he's afraid he'll miss out on midnight snacks

1. My dog Riley rarely goes to bed early; _____.
2. Jesamine is not a very sociable cat; _____.
3. Harry the Hamster entertains himself; _____.
4. I keep Harry's cage far from Slinky's; _____.
5. I don't know where my tarantula is; _____.

Directions: Each of the following sentences is missing a semicolon. Insert the semicolon in the appropriate place.

6. Ron's birthday is on Saturday he plans to spend the day at the beach.
7. The Student Council made three recommendations only one was accepted.
8. Some people like pizza with a thick crust others prefer theirs thin and crisp.
9. Mr. Vinson spends hours in his garden every week it takes time to make plants flourish.
10. The children got a toy robot on Tuesday by Saturday morning, it was in pieces.

Name: _____ **Date:** _____

A hyphen (-) has several uses.

USE	EXAMPLE
join parts of compound numbers	twenty-nine
join two words that work as one adjective before a noun	a pure-bred poodle a well-known artist
divide a word at the end of a line	The dishes served at the ban-quet included lasagna and green bean salad.
separate the word parts in some compound words	sister-in-law half-baked

Directions: Rewrite the sentences, using hyphens wherever possible. If the sentence contains a word that is divided, insert a hyphen at the division. Use a dictionary to check what compound words require hyphens.

1. At the age of sixty seven, the best selling author built a mansion on a tropical island.

2. You can freeze the half baked pie and finish baking it in a hot oven for twenty five minutes.

3. Great Aunt Nora showed a lot of self control when she spoke softly to the naughty child.

4. The mild mannered reporter dashed to the phone booth to change into his famous blue tights and red cape.

5. Although he is only fifty five, Brandon's father in law has snow white hair.

Name: _____ Date: _____

The dash (—) is a bold piece of punctuation. It requires readers to stop—and then continue. Dashes are longer than hyphens. They can be used either singly or in pairs, and they have many uses. Read the examples below.

To mark an unexpected break in thought
I'm okay with that idea—at least for now.
The Labor Day Festival—the only one in the area worth going to—is next weekend.

To set off examples
School supplies—notebooks, pens, pencils, calculators—can be found in aisle 8.

To set off an appositive when commas may be confusing
The article discussed the economies of several northern countries—Greenland, Iceland, Norway, and Sweden—and their environmental issues.

To indicate hesitation in speech
"I—I'm pretty sure we're lost," Freda whispered.

Dashes are considered to be "casual" punctuation, so be careful not to overuse them in your formal writing.

Directions: The following sentences are missing one or two dashes. Use proofreading marks to insert them in the correct places.

1. I love the style of this jacket I just hate the color.

2. The three dogs Reddy, Rufus, and Bear lazed about in the noonday sun.

3. We're studying the Incas how they lived, what they believed, etc. in this unit.

4. It's not that Dorie hates cats she's just a little afraid of them.

5. Ethan had just finished making a huge sandwich then he dropped it on the floor.

Directions: Complete the following sentences by adding information either after the single dash or between the double dashes. For number 10, write a line of dialogue in which the speaker hesitates in his or her speech.

6. It's June—_____—and I'm sick in bed with a cold.

7. That math test was easy—_____.

8. Computers are great—_____.

9. Our new products—_____—can now be purchased from our web site!

10. _____
_____

USING PARENTHESES

Parentheses are used in a sentence to enclose extra information that is not essential to the meaning of the sentence. If the parentheses come at the end of the sentence, put the punctuation outside the last parenthesis.

Three World War I biplanes (now out of commission) will be open to the public during the air show.

The air show will be held at Simmons Airfield (close to the airport).

If the information is an exclamation or a question, include the end mark inside the parentheses. If it is a statement, do not include the period.

My friend Paul (have you met him before?) goes to Mayberry Junior High School.

You can borrow my copy of Little House on the Prairie (I've read it three times).

Directions: Rewrite each sentence, adding parentheses and punctuation where needed.

1. My uncle the one who lives in Canada is coming for a visit next week.

_____

2. Payne Preston is he a friend of yours invited me to his party.

_____

3. The thieves got away with the money about $10,000 in small bills.

_____

4. My first day on my new computer, I sent an email to Paige she's my cousin.

_____

5. Mr. Mason used the story of Cinderella poor girl strikes it rich by marrying a prince to show that one's lot in life can change suddenly.

_____

6. The steep Rocky Mountains now paved with highways prevented many pioneers from reaching the West.

_____

7. Three of my four cousins have volunteered at the hospital the fourth was too young to volunteer.

_____

8. The storms you'll be thrilled to hear this will end tonight.

_____

9. The car's paint job neon green and black made people stop and stare.

_____

10. What you really should do although you probably won't agree is find a new topic for your project.

_____

Name: _____   Date: _____

Occasionally when writing, you may include extra information in information that is already in parentheses. When this happens, enclose this information within brackets ([]) inside the parentheses.

> Some German words (such as *Gesundheit* [said after a sneeze]) have become part of the English language.

Brackets may also be used to enclose the pronunciation of a word.

> The word *Gesundheit* [geh-zoont-hite] is a wish for good health to the person who sneezed.

Brackets are also used to enclose stage directions in a script.

> JIM [grabbing a tissue] Ah-choo! [He blows his nose] Excuse me.

Directions: Add brackets to each sentence where needed.

1. The rufous-sided towhee (so named for its call a clear *to-wheee*) lives in thickets and brushy woods.

2. Exercise can improve a person's physique fizz-eek, or body shape.

3. Texas's Chisholm Trail (named after Jesse Chisholm 1806–1868) ran from San Antonio to Abilene.

4. The first step in making spinach soufflé is to wash and coarsely chop one pound of fresh spinach (you can substitute one package of frozen spinach thaw it in the microwave first).

5. A *facade* fah-sahd is the front of a building or the front, false or real, that people present to others.

Directions: Add brackets where need to this script excerpt.

MRS. WHIGGINS *Looking puzzled*
> I just can't understand what happened to my lovely pie. I set it right here to cool just an hour ago.

DODIE *Shaking head and looking serious*
> That IS strange. She glances down and quickly brushes crumbs off her shirt Where could it have gone?

Sentences need two parts to make a complete thought. The subject tells *who* or *what.* The predicate tells what the subject *is* or *does.*

A complete subject is made up of all the words in the subject. A complete predicate is all the words that make up the predicate. Complete subjects and complete predicates may be a single word or groups of words.

┌── COMPLETE SUBJECT ──┐	┌── COMPLETE PREDICATE ──┐
Mrs. Gunderson	teaches history.
Her history quiz games	are always fun to play.
Andy and Marcus	are two of her students.

Directions: Draw a line between the complete subject and the complete predicate of each sentence.

1. Many Japanese immigrants arrived in the United States around the 1900's.

2. Most were single young men.

3. Almost none were single young women.

4. The young men wanted wives.

5. They wrote letters to the matchmakers in their villages back in Japan.

6. They described themselves in the letters.

7. The matchmaker would locate a suitable young woman.

8. She would then send a picture of the woman to the prospective groom.

9. The groom would approve or disapprove the choice.

10. Most approved of the brides the matchmaker found for them.

11. From 1900 to 1920, 20,000 "picture brides" came to the U.S.

12. Many of these brides were happy with their new husbands.

13. Others were disappointed.

14. Their husbands had exaggerated the success they had found in America.

15. Their husbands were simply poor laborers.

16. The brides faced miserable living conditions in the new land.

17. They faced language barriers and discrimination.

18. Some of these disappointed women returned to Japan.

19. But most stayed and made the best of their situation.

20. They worked with their husbands in the fields, raised families, and did what they could to ensure a good future for their children.

Name: _____   **Date:** _____

A complete subject is made up of all the words in the subject. It can be one word or a group of words. The main word in a complete subject is called the **simple subject**.

<u>Those large black birds over there</u> must be crows.

In this sentence, *Those large black birds over there* is the complete subject. The simple subject is *birds. Birds* is the main word of the complete subject.

<u>Professor Henry Higgins</u> studies languages.

Sometimes the simple subject is several words that name a person or place. In this sentence, *Professor Henry Higgins* is the simple subject.

Directions: Underline the simple subject in each sentence.

1. The crab fisherman's boat sank during the storm.
2. Max Wedgerman draws great landscapes.
3. The letter you wrote to the newspaper should be sent today.
4. The orange tabby cat carried her kittens out of the barn.
5. The first recipe in this book calls for jalapeño peppers.
6. A red and white striped towel was left behind at the swimming pool.
7. The music on this radio station is very relaxing.
8. David's baseball glove smells of dirt and leather.
9. The delicate blue dragonfly hovered over the alfalfa field.
10. Milo's piano sounds out of tune.
11. That out-of-print book by the late Jack London is very costly.
12. Jaycee, my best friend, loves animals.
13. The library that was built last year is on the east side of town.
14. The principal of the middle school met with the teachers.
15. Mindy's favorite shoes got ruined in the rain.

Directions: Complete each sentence by adding a complete subject. Then draw a circle around the simple subject in each complete subject you write.

16. _____ has chewed a hole in the cereal box.
17. _____ dashed off an angry letter to the editor.
18. _____ snaked through the canyon.
19. _____ should try harder next time.
20. _____ usually costs a lot.

Name: _____   **Date:** _____

An imperative sentence gives an order. The subject is always *you*. It is not stated in the sentence. *You* is an "understood" subject.

Be careful. (Who should be careful? You.)

To find the simple subject of an interrogative sentence, reword the question into a statement. Then ask yourself whom or what the sentence is about.

Does anyone want to come with me? (<u>Anyone</u> wants to come with me.)

Directions: Write the simple subject of each sentence.

1. What does this button do? _____

2. Don't touch it. _____

3. Can we play on this computer? _____

4. Leave it alone! _____

5. Does anyone know how to open this program?

_____

6. Type in the password. _____

7. Why doesn't this work? _____

8. Did someone break it already? _____

9. Tell me who did this. _____

10. Confess! _____

Directions: Rewrite each sentence, changing it to the type of sentence indicated in parentheses. Then write the simple subject of the sentence you wrote.

11. I wonder who broke the computer. (Interrogative)

_____ Simple subject: _____

12. You shouldn't play with this equipment. (Imperative)

_____ Simple subject: _____

13. Perhaps someone can fix it for you. (Interrogative)

_____ Simple subject: _____

14. You should put a lock on your door. (Imperative)

_____ Simple subject: _____

15. Perhaps that will solve the problem. (Interrogative)

_____ Simple subject: _____

Name: _____ **Date:** _____

 Language Arts Skills & Strategies, Level 7 • Saddleback Publishing, Inc. ©2005 • 3 Watson, Irvine, CA 92618 • Phone (888) 735-2225 • www.sdlback.com

The complete predicate of a sentence is the word or group of words that tells what the subject does. The simple predicate is the main verb in a complete predicate.

The seventh grade class **planned** a class trip together.

In this sentence, *planned a class trip together* is the complete predicate. The simple predicate is *planned*.

The students **have been looking** forward to it.

A simple predicate may be made up of more than one word. In this sentence, it is made up of the helping verbs *have been* and the main verb *looking*.

Directions: Write the simple predicate in each sentence.

1. Shaquille has written a note to his coach. _____

2. Mari has found a wallet on the sidewalk. _____

3. Mr. Zeco has been living in the U.S. for several years. _____

4. The princess will become a great queen someday. _____

5. Libby and her friends have been dancing all night. _____

6. Ms. Manfredi will be giving guitar lessons this summer. _____

7. My grandparents exercise every day. _____

8. The mole burrowed his way through the flower bed. _____

9. The flock of geese spends time at our pond on its way south. _____

10. Duff will be an excellent tenor soon. _____

11. The Hawks have lost several tournaments in the last few years. _____

12. Last week Mrs. Ramirez opened an account at the bank. _____

13. Mr. Connors was once a counselor at Medgars Middle School. _____

14. The two lead dogs lugged the sled through a foot of new snow. _____

15. That car had been running fine until now. _____

Directions: Complete each sentence by adding a complete predicate. Draw a circle around the simple predicate in each complete predicate you write.

16. Most of my friends _____

17. The new mall _____

18. Some teenagers _____

19. The swimming pool _____

20. A tiny dog _____

Name: _____   **Date:** _____

You have learned that the main word in a complete subject is called the simple subject. A **compound subject** has two or more simple subjects joined by the connecting word *and* or *or*. There may be other words between the subjects. The subjects have the same predicate.

Troy and the other children laughed at the clown.

The compound subject here is *Troy* and *children*. The subjects share the simple predicate *laughed*.

Directions: Underline the sentences that have a compound subject.

Alexis, Aleesha, and Amber are triplets.

All three play the violin.

This morning, a hummingbird and a sphinx moth visited my petunias.

Those books need to be returned to the library.

The audience was eager for the show to begin.

That desk and that gray cabinet should be moved into the den.

Seven boys and five girls signed up for the basketball camp.

All the counselors are professional players.

Did Maggie, Patrick, and Tristan all have birthdays last week?

This evening, Carl and his family are coming over for dinner.

A nice bath or a shower would feel good right now.

My favorite colors are red and black.

Football, soccer, and golf are Thad's favorite sports.

The books, candles, greeting cards, and figurines on that table are on sale today.

Mario, Diana, Suzette, and I watched the lightning from the safety of the living room.

Directions: Add a compound subject to the following predicates. Use *and* or *or* to join the subjects.

1. _____ need to be taken for a walk.

2. Do _____ have homework to do?

3. Will _____ start at the same time?

4. _____ crawled into the closet.

5. _____ are full of holes.

Name: _____   Date: _____

The main word in a complete predicate is called the simple predicate. A **compound predicate** has two or more simple predicates, joined by the connecting word *and* or *or.* The predicates have the same subject.

Enrique <u>plays</u> the saxophone in the jazz band and <u>runs</u> track.

The compound predicate here is *plays* and *runs.* The verbs share the subject *Enrique.*

Next year he <u>will work</u> on the school newspaper or <u>join</u> the drama club.

In this sentence, the compound predicate is *will work* and *join.*

Directions: Underline the sentences that have a compound predicate.

Brenda received many compliments on her new haircut.

The cat jumped out of Tamari's arms and ran out of the room.

That faucet has been dripping since before we moved in here.

Hector got goosebumps and his hair stood on end.

This tool can be used to core apples.

Either open the window or turn on that fan.

Victor has tried mountain climbing and bungee jumping.

My head feels like it's being pounded with a hammer!

Can you do a back flip off the high dive?

Manny and Carrie will fold and put away the laundry.

Directions: Add a compound predicate to the following subjects. Use *and* or *or* to join the predicates.

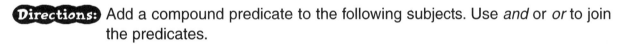

1. Jake and Jillian _____.

2. The rusty old tractor _____.

3. The puppies _____.

4. Anthony's mother _____.

5. The old woman _____.

Name: _____ **Date:** _____

DIRECT OBJECTS

Some sentences tell a complete thought with only two parts, a subject and a verb.

Charles sneezed.

Other sentences include a direct object. A direct object is a noun or pronoun that receives the action of the verb. It answers the question *What?* or *Whom?* about the verb.

Winnie carried the **basket** and her **backpack** upstairs.
(What did she carry upstairs? basket and backpack)

Notice that a direct object can be compound (basket and backpack).

Directions: Underline the direct object or objects in each sentence.

1. I have a headache and my back hurts.
2. Moles often destroy yards and gardens.
3. Amanda left her jacket and hat on the bus today.
4. Would you rather watch this video or that show?
5. The caterpillar had green stripes, yellow dots, and bright orange horns.
6. While Simon read the recipe aloud, Anne chopped the parsley.
7. That comedian made me laugh so hard!
8. Georgie swept up the broken glass and put it in the trashcan.
9. The boys stayed up late, telling jokes and trading stories.
10. Too much water will kill a cactus, and not enough will damage roses.

Directions: Provide a direct object for each of the following sentences.

11. Mrs. Mendenhall sang _____ while she cooked.
12. Georgette brought _____ to school.
13. The scout leader told _____ while they hiked.
14. Layla ordered _____ to go with her wallpaper.
15. Stephen sent _____ back to the company.
16. Andy located _____ on the map.
17. The critic gave _____ a "thumbs down."
18. Mrs. Harkin dictated _____ to her secretary.
19. The software program protected _____ from viruses.
20. The horse pulled _____ through the field.

Name: _____   **Date:** _____

Some sentences have two kinds of objects, direct and indirect. As you have learned, the direct object receives the action of the verb. The indirect object tells for whom or to whom the action is done. Indirect objects always come before direct objects.

> Mr. Mertz gave his **wife** a bracelet. (*Wife* receives the direct object, *bracelet*.)
> Byron taught his **dog** a trick. (*Dog* receives the direct object, *trick*.)

To determine if a verb has an indirect object, ask yourself *"to or for whom?"* or *"to or for what?"* about the verb. The answer is the indirect object.

> Mia told April and me a good joke. (Told to whom? *April* and *me*)

Indirect objects never follow the words *to* or *for*.

> Mia told a good joke **to** <u>April and me</u>. (No indirect object)

Directions: Provide an indirect object for each of the following sentences.

1. The horse gave _____ a nudge with its nose.
2. Pass _____ the sugar, please.
3. Inez lent _____ five dollars.
4. Mrs. Jimenez baked _____ a special dessert.
5. Zachariah left _____ a note.
6. The realtor found _____ the house of their dreams.
7. "Save _____ some popcorn or he'll be mad," Bart said.
8. "You owe _____ a dollar," Martin reminded his sister.
9. Barney offered _____ a ride to the mall.
10. The runner handed _____ the baton.

Directions: Each of the following sentences has one direct object. Some of them also have an indirect object. Underline the direct objects. Circle the indirect objects.

11. Julius showed us his stamp collection.
12. The babysitter taught the children a new game to play.
13. Simon told the secret to everyone.
14. The rosebush dropped its petals on the pavement.
15. The black cat lurking in the shadows gave Helen and Rico a fright!
16. A pinch of cinnamon gives this sauce a special flavor.
17. This path will lead visitors to the bamboo garden.
18. The students gave their finished projects to the teacher.
19. Subir asks his brother many questions about his job.
20. The art teacher explained the process to the students.

Name: _____ **Date:** _____

A noun is a person, place, thing, or idea. The nouns in the following sentences are underlined.

The <u>chilliness</u> of the <u>water</u> at <u>Spider Lake Park</u> made <u>Marlise</u> shiver as she swam.

People	Places	Things	Ideas
Marlise	Spider Lake Park	water	chilliness

A noun can consist of more than one word.

The United States   Mr. Lopez   merry-go-round

Nouns that name things that you can see, hear, touch, taste, or smell are called concrete nouns. Nouns that name ideas, qualities, or feelings are called abstract nouns.

Concrete: water, park, Marlise, apple, street, guitar, dog
Abstract: chilliness, amazement, anger, love, mystery

Directions: Label each noun *Concrete* or *Abstract*.

1. chair _____
2. health _____
3. friendship _____
4. turtle _____
5. Fred _____

6. carpet _____
7. bathtub _____
8. confusion _____
9. elbow _____
10. history _____

Directions: Underline the nouns in the following sentences. Write each in the appropriate column in the chart.

CONCRETE	ABSTRACT

11. Victor has little tolerance for other people's bad behavior.

12. A feeling of sadness came over us when the boat pulled away from the shore.

13. Justine brushed one last layer of paint on the birdhouse she made in class.

14. It's important to have patience and determination while learning to play the piano.

15. George let out a cry of pain when the encyclopedia landed on his toe.

Name: _____   **Date:** _____

A **common noun** is a noun that names any person, place, thing, or idea. A **proper noun** names a particular person, place, thing, or idea. Proper nouns should always begin with a capital letter. If a proper noun consists of more than one word, capitalize the important words only.

Common Nouns: city   movie   river   month

Proper Nouns: St. Louis   The Wizard of Oz   Snake River   June

A **collective noun** is one that names a group.

audience   team   bunch   herd   swarm   crew

A **compound noun** is one that is made up of two or more words. The words may be joined as one, hyphenated, or separate from each other.

daytime   father-in-law   Amy-Jo   telephone pole   Sam Smith

Directions: Write proper or common nouns to finish the chart. Be sure to capitalize the proper nouns. One of them has been done for you.

COMMON NOUN	PROPER NOUN
EXAMPLE: holiday	Valentine's Day
1.	Utah
2. restaurant	
3.	Griffin High School
4.	Museum of Modern Art
5. planet	
6.	China
7. song	
8.	Rocky Mountains
9. writer	
10. day	

Directions: Label each noun by writing *Common* or *Proper* on the line. Then, if the noun is compound, write *Compound,* and if it is collective, write *Collective.*

11. hotel _____

12. New York Yankees _____

13. brother _____

14. family _____

15. New Hampshire _____

Name: _____   **Date:** _____

A **singular noun** names only one person, place, or thing. A **plural noun** names more than one. Follow these rules for forming plural nouns.

Most singular nouns	Add –s.	letter–letters shoe–shoes
Nouns that end in –ch, –x, –sh, or –s	Add –es.	birch–birches Jones–Joneses
Nouns that end in a vowel and y	Add –s.	day–days monkey–monkeys
Nouns that end in a consonant and y	Change y to i and add –ies.	penny–pennies lady–ladies
Family names that end in y	Add –s.	Mr. Gantry–the Gantrys
Nouns that end in –f or –fe	Change f or fe to v and add –es to some.	life–lives leaf–leaves
	Add –s to others.	gulf–gulfs cliff–cliffs

Directions: Write the plural form of each noun. Use a dictionary if you need help.

1. self _____
2. cherry _____
3. staff _____
4. mess _____
5. novel _____

6. wife _____
7. latch _____
8. roof _____
9. Murphy _____
10. ash _____

Directions: Some of these plural nouns were formed incorrectly. If the noun is spelled correctly, write *Correct.* If it is incorrect, write it correctly. Use a dictionary to check your answers.

11. prizes _____
12. monkies _____
13. thiefs _____
14. the Bells _____
15. circuses _____
16. spys _____
17. leafs _____
18. batchs _____

19. knives _____
20. foxes _____
21. bodies _____
22. hoofs _____
23. the Bradies _____
24. waves _____
25. halfs _____

When you are not sure how to spell a plural form of a noun, check in a dictionary.

Singular nouns that end in *–o* have special rules.

Nouns that end in a vowel plus *o*	Add *–s*.	radio–radios rodeo–rodeos
Nouns that end in a consonant plus *o*	Add *–es* to some.	potato–potatoes tomato–tomatoes
	Add *–s* to others.	video–videos pro–pros memo–memos
Family names and music-related words that end in *o*	Add *–s* to most	solo–solos piano–pianos Mrs. Trevino–the Trevinos

There are special rules for forming the plural of compound nouns. Compound nouns written as one word are made plural by adding to or changing the last part of the compound.

doghouse—doghouses   stepchild—stepchildren

Hyphenated nouns or two-word nouns are made plural by adding to or changing the most important part of the compound.

leap year—leap years   runner-up—runners-up

Directions: Write the plural form of each noun. Use a dictionary to check your spelling.

1. sister-in-law _____

2. volcano _____

3. studio _____

4. sidewalk _____

5. Delgado _____

6. cello _____

7. igloo _____

8. torpedo _____

9. ice floe _____

10. truck driver _____

11. Caruso _____

12. solo _____

13. alto _____

14. potato _____

15. passer-by _____

16. banjo _____

17. zero _____

18. piano _____

19. seventh-grader _____

20. echo _____

Name: _____   **Date:** _____

Most nouns are made plural by adding *–s* or *–es*, but some nouns do not follow this rule. The best way to learn the plural forms of such nouns is to simply memorize them.

Some nouns have special plural forms.

child—children	foot—feet	goose—geese
louse—lice	man—men	ox—oxen

Some nouns do not change at all in the plural. Their singular and plural forms are the same.

deer—deer	fish—fish	sheep—sheep	moose—moose

Some nouns are always plural and have no singular form.

jeans	trousers	oats	measles	mumps
scissors	shears	tongs	tweezers	pliers

There are some nouns that are normally never used in the plural. They are called *mass* or *non-count* nouns because they cannot be counted in the way other nouns, such as *apples* or *lakes,* can.

advice	software	homework	cotton	dirt	gold
silver	copper	sugar	wheat	corn	milk

Directions: Write the correct form of the noun in parentheses. Use a dictionary if you need help.

1. In Canada, we saw several (moose) _____.

2. Use those (tongs) _____ to turn the steaks on the grill.

3. I have English and math (homework) _____ tonight.

4. That sentence should be enclosed in (parenthesis) _____.

5. The counselor offered a lot of (advice) _____ to the students.

6. Shelley is wearing black (jeans) _____ today.

7. The (oats) _____ are in that bin.

8. My dad has a pair of (pliers) _____ for every task.

9. You'll find the (sugar) _____ in aisle 6.

10. Reggie looked at two (louse) _____ under a microscope.

11. The team of (ox) _____ pulled the plow through the dirt.

12. Did you catch any (fish) _____ today?

13. The farm workers sheared the (wool) _____ off all the (sheep) _____.

14. The veterinarian had to pull three of the dog's (tooth) _____.

15. The thief gathered up all the (gold) _____ and (silver) _____.

Name: _____ **Date:** _____

Possessive nouns show that someone or something has or owns something. Follow these rules to form possessive nouns:
- Add –'s to singular nouns: *a bird's wings*
- Add –' to plural nouns ending in –s: *the boys' room*
- Add –'s to plural nouns that do not end in –s: *children's toys*

Directions: Write the possessive form of the noun or nouns in parentheses on the lines.

1. the _____ engine (car)

2. the _____ cover (magazine)

3. these _____ architect (houses)

4. _____ skills (Charles)

5. the _____ hiding place (mice)

6. the _____ handles (pliers)

7. the _____ locker room (men)

8. _____ design (Tom)

9. an _____ entertainment (evening)

10. one _____ worth of candy (dollar)

11. one _____ project (girl)

12. _____ cell phone (Mara)

13. those _____ concerns (neighbors)

14. three _____ attendance charts (teachers)

15. a full _____ work (day)

16. those _____ careers (actors)

17. the _____ car (Browns)

18. those _____ lives (people)

19. the _____ babies (fox)

20. the _____ calls (moose)

Directions: Rewrite each phrase to use a possessive noun.

21. the lobby of the hotel _____

22. the effort of one month _____

23. the flashlight that belongs to Anne _____

24. the health of the dog _____

25. the responsibility of Phyllis _____

26. the wigs the opera singers wear _____

27. the pay of one hour _____

28. the skateboards of the teens _____

29. a roar of a lion _____

30. the car of Mr. Evans _____

Name: _____   **Date:** _____

Sometimes two or more individuals share ownership of something. For joint ownership of something, add –'s or –' only to the owner that is named last in the sentence.

> Chelsea and Daryl's teacher is Mr. Gonzales.
> (Chelsea and Daryl have the same teacher.)

Sometimes two or more individuals each own something without sharing ownership. For example, two children may each have a red ballcap. To express this type of ownership, add –'s to each owner.

> Blake's and Thea's notebooks are falling apart.
> (Blake owns one notebook, and Thea owns another.)

Directions: Rewrite each sentence, adding –'s –', or nothing to the underlined nouns to show the kind of ownership indicated in parentheses.

1. My <u>aunt</u> and <u>uncle</u> house is cozy. (They own the house together.)

   _____

2. <u>Cheyenne</u>, <u>Gavin</u>, and <u>Melissa</u> project is on ecosystems. (The three students worked on the project together.)

   _____

3. <u>New York</u> and <u>Maryland</u> school systems were part of the study. (Each state has its own school system.)

   _____

4. The <u>third grade</u> and <u>fourth grade</u> lunch period is at 11:40. (Both grades share the lunch period.)

   _____

5. The representatives debated lowering the <u>highway</u> and <u>interstate</u> speed limits. (Each has its own speed limits.)

   _____

6. <u>Louise</u> and <u>Emma</u> last name is Lamanski. (The girls are in the same family.)

   _____

7. <u>Houston</u> and <u>Dallas</u> pro football teams draw huge crowds. (Each city has its own pro football team.)

   _____

8. The <u>dog</u> and <u>cat</u> owner was unaware of the leash law. (The dog and cat have the same owner.)

   _____

Name: _____   **Date:** _____

A noun is the name of a person, place, thing, or idea. A pronoun is a word that takes the place of a noun. The noun that is replaced is called the antecedent. The antecedent may be in the same sentence as the pronoun, or in a different sentence.

A pronoun must agree in number with its antecedent. Singular pronouns replace singular antecedents. Plural pronouns replace plural antecedents.

SENTENCE	PRONOUN	ANTECEDENT
Last week, **Simon** coached **his** little sister's soccer team.	his	Simon
He showed the **players** new ways to improve **their** techniques.	He their	Simon players
They appreciated his help.	They his	players Simon

Directions: Circle the antecedent of each underlined pronoun.

1. The team practices at Zilker Park. <u>It</u> is open until 10:00 p.m.

2. There are twelve players on the team. <u>They</u> will get new T-shirts this week.

3. Simon got Cousin Sylvie to coach the team with <u>him</u>.

4. Sylvie and Simon enjoyed <u>their</u> time with the children.

5. <u>They</u> listened carefully to the advice Sylvie gave.

Directions: Underline each pronoun. Draw an arrow to its antecedent.

6. Simon grabbed a ball from the equipment bag. It needed more air.

7. Simon blew it up, and then checked the others to see if they needed air, too.

8. Sylvie tossed the balls to the players. They practiced passing them from player to player.

9. When Lonnie scored a goal in the first five minutes of the game, Simon couldn't believe his eyes!

10. Lonnie and all the players gained a lot from their time with Simon and Sylvie.

Name: _____ Date: _____

It is not always easy to decide what pronoun goes with an antecedent. Read the guidelines for pronoun/antecedent agreement that follow.

- Two singular antecedents joined by *and* usually take a plural pronoun.
  <u>Jalon and Leon</u> rode **their** bikes to the park.
- *Each* and *every* are singular and require singular pronouns.
  <u>Every</u> student should bring **his or her** book to music class.
- Two singular antecedents joined by *or, either/or,* or *neither/nor* are treated separately and require singular pronouns.
  <u>Either Jillian or Ronda</u> has **her** cell phone with **her**.
- One singular and one plural antecedent joined by *and* require a plural pronoun.
  <u>Ritchie and the other basketball players</u> led **their** classmates in the victory yell.

Directions: Each sentence contains an incorrect pronoun. Rewrite each correctly.

1. The cows and the horse found its way to the barn during the blizzard.

   _____

2. Each of the puppies will be given their own bed.

   _____

3. The scouts used his compasses to find their way out of the woods.

   _____

4. Neither Becky nor Christina has seen their artwork in the gallery yet.

   _____

5. The teammates donated its jerseys to the auction.

   _____

6. The giraffe stretched their long neck out to nibble the highest leaves.

   _____

7. Every pet needs to have their shots and heartworm treatment on time.

   _____

8. Either Ricky or Martin will bring their guitar to music class tomorrow.

   _____

9. A hiker without a map could easily lose their way.

   _____

10. Peg and Tess stowed her backpacks under the bench.

   _____

Name: _____   **Date:** _____

The subject of a sentence is who or what the sentence is about. Subject pronouns can take the place of nouns used as subjects of sentences.

Linda and **I** are hungry.   **We** are hungry.

Subject pronouns can also follow forms of the verb *be*.

The fastest runners are **Allen** and **Beth**. The fastest runners are **they**.

The pronouns *me, you, him, her, it, us,* and *them* are object pronouns. They come after action verbs and prepositions such as *to, for, in, at,* and *with*.

Give the note to **Christina**.   Give the note to **her**.

SUBJECT PRONOUNS	
Singular	**Plural**
I	we
you	you
he, she, it	they

OBJECT PRONOUNS	
Singular	**Plural**
me	us
you	you
him, her, it	them

Directions: Write the pronoun that can replace the underlined word or words.

1. <u>George and Rebecca</u> take French horn lessons. _____

2. <u>Mr. Lennon</u> received a phone call from the school nurse last night. _____

3. Molly fixed <u>her bike</u> while the three cats watched idly. _____

4. Mr. McRoberts read <u>the articles</u> to us just before lunch time. _____

5. The counselors' meeting will focus on <u>the student's concerns</u>. _____

6. <u>My friends and I</u> usually meet at the mall. _____

7. This is the biggest of <u>all the pumpkins</u>. _____

8. Most of <u>the cake</u> was eaten by the time I arrived at the party. _____

9. I got a ride to rehearsal with <u>Ms. Lamprey</u>. _____

10. <u>Tom's mother</u> works in the same building as my mom. _____

Directions: Choose the correct pronoun in parentheses. Write it on the line.

11. Ms. Treece assigned _____ (we/us) two chapters to read tonight.

12. When Donna handed _____ (I/me) the note, I put it in my pocket.

13. The only person who didn't see the movie was _____ (she/her).

14. _____ (They/Them) left on their trip two days ago.

15. Maybe Yoshi will lend _____ (I/me) her red pen.

Name: _____   **Date:** _____

A compound subject is two or more simple subjects joined by *and* or *or.* Be sure that any pronoun used as a subject in a compound subject is a subject pronoun.

Incorrect: Mia and me like ballet.

Correct: Mia and I like ballet.

Use this simple test to check that the correct pronoun has been used. Remove *Mia* from the first sentence. It is not correct to say, "Me like ballet." It is correct to say, "I like ballet." Therefore, it is also correct to say "Mia and I like ballet."

You have also learned to use object pronouns after action verbs and words such as *to, for, in, at,* and *with.* Be sure to use object pronouns in compound objects.

Andy asked Daniel and me a question.

You can use the same test to check that you have used an object pronoun correctly. Remove Daniel from the sentence. It is correct to say, "Andy asked me a question." Therefore, it is also correct to say "Andy asked Daniel and me a question."

When you use *I* or *me* with other nouns or pronouns, always name yourself last.

My family and I went camping. The ones who had the most fun were my sister and me.

Directions: Choose the pronoun that correctly completes each sentence. Write the pronoun on the line.

1. Megan and _____ signed up to volunteer at the senior center. (I/me)

2. Tory and _____ are always the first ones finished. (he/him)

3. Allow Stacy and _____ to have a turn, please. (I/me)

4. The Thompsons and _____ often have dinner together. (we/us)

5. Grandpa built Barbie and _____ a playhouse when we were younger. (I/me)

6. The teacher said that Randy and _____ speak excellent Spanish. (she/her)

7. Mr. Ha gave Carla and _____ a chance to do extra credit. (they/them)

8. The principal asked Lynn and _____ to help the new students. (we/us)

9. My first choice for class treasurer is either Shawna or _____. (he/him)

10. The last guests to leave were the Smiths and _____. (they/them)

11. Marcus and _____ served as ushers at the concert. (I/me)

12. Nobody remembers if the winner of the match was Brant or _____. (she/her)

13. Are the children going to ride with Mrs. Stallings and _____? (he/him)

14. Oscar and Lucy's favorite babysitters are Hannah and _____. (she/her)

15. It seems like Anthony and _____ really enjoyed this book. (they, them)

Name: _____   **Date:** _____

Pronouns that end in *–self* or *–selves* are reflexive pronouns. A reflexive pronoun always refers to the subject of a predicate. Using a reflexive pronoun indicates that the subject both performs and receives the action of the verb.

Kyle dusted himself off and got back on the horse.

REFLEXIVE PRONOUNS	
Singular	**Plural**
myself	ourselves
yourself	yourselves
himself, herself, itself	themselves

Never use a reflexive pronoun when you can use a subject or object pronoun.

Incorrect	**Correct**
The Sanjabis and **myself** *were on time.*	The Sanjabis and **I** were on time.

Directions: Provide a reflexive pronoun for each of the following sentences.

1. Students who don't put forth an effort are only hurting _____.

2. You gave _____ a haircut?

3. Ellen and Hector bought _____ a new computer.

4. Gina could have kicked _____ for losing her new bracelet!

5. Keenu wants to get _____ out of debt as soon as possible.

6. We should remind _____ of the important things in life.

7. "Ask _____ if the two of you want to take on such a big job," said Mr. Olson to the boys.

8. "Pour _____ some orange juice," Grandma told Valerie.

9. Michael hit _____ in the foot when he dropped the bat.

10. Kayla is always feeling sorry for _____.

11. The three bluebirds were preening _____ on a branch.

12. This package was sent to Pete and _____.

13. Marco admitted that the sender of the note was _____.

14. These plates are so shiny that you can see _____.

15. We can let _____ into the cabin with the hidden key.

Name: _____ **Date:** _____

Possessive pronouns show ownership. There are two forms of possessive pronouns. Some are always followed by a noun. Others always stand on their own.

POSSESSIVE PRONOUNS USED WITH NOUNS		EXAMPLES
my	our	May I borrow **your pencil?**
his, her, its	their	**My pen** just ran out.
your	your	

POSSESSIVE PRONOUNS THAT STAND ALONE		EXAMPLES
mine	ours	This green marker is **mine**.
his, hers, its	theirs	Which paints are **yours**?
yours	yours	**Hers** are in the supply closet.

Notice that *his* and *its* can be used with nouns and can also stand alone.

I found **his** paintbrushes.   **His** need to be cleaned.

Do not confuse the possessive pronouns *its*, *their*, and *your* with the contractions *it's*, *they're*, and *you're*. Remember, possessive pronouns never use apostrophes.

Directions: Underline the word that correctly completes each sentence.

1. Is that (my, mine) dollar bill under your foot?

2. That scarf is (your, yours), isn't it?

3. "(Hers, Her) cost too much," Mrs. Phoenix remarked, speaking about the vendor's candles.

4. (You're, Your) letter really impressed the boss.

5. Santiago gave (he's, his) brother a high-five at the end of the game.

6. "(Yours, Your) is the nicest house on the block," Katrina said.

7. The two Arabian horses are (theirs, their, theirs').

8. The choice is (ours, our): we can sit and do nothing, or jump in and enjoy life.

9. Reggie picked up the laundry basket and dumped (it's, its) contents on the bed.

10. "(Ours, Our, Ours') is the yard with all the wildflowers," Mrs. Coy said.

11. That series is in (its, it's, its') fourth season already.

12. "The responsibility to submit the application is (her, hers, hers')," the counselor told the parents.

13. "(Your, Yours) is the only pizza I like," Ken told his mother.

14. A cricket sings by rubbing (its, it's) wings together.

15. "The fault is all (mine, my)," Aubrey confessed.

Name: _____   **Date:** _____

Most pronouns refer to particular people, places, or things. Indefinite pronouns do not refer to particular nouns. Some take singular verbs. Others take plural verbs. Some can take singular or plural verbs, depending on the situation.

COMMON INDEFINITE PRONOUNS			
Singular	anybody somebody everyone anyone someone each anything something either nobody everybody neither nothing everything		**Everybody is** in the living room. **Nothing has** happened here. **Each has** a lollipop. **Neither** telephone **works.**
Plural	both many several few others		**Many hope** to play on the team. **Few have** tried out. **Several** need more practice.
Singular or Plural	all none some any most		**All** of the water **is** polluted. **All** of the banks **are** closed. **Some** of the money **is** missing. **Some** of the pens **are** out of ink.

Directions: Underline the indefinite pronoun in each sentence. Write *Singular* if the pronoun is singular. Write *Plural* if the pronoun is plural.

1. Everybody needs to share an idea with the group. _____
2. All the chips are nacho flavored. _____
3. Somebody has left her purse in the classroom. _____
4. Each of the boys is responsible for his own possessions. _____
5. Neither of the girls speaks Spanish. _____
6. Many have come to see the fireworks. _____
7. Most of the salesclerks are busy right now. _____
8. Few people were able to come to the block party. _____
9. One of the jury members disagrees with the head juror. _____
10. Several of the animals have escaped from their cages. _____

Directions: Underline the verb that correctly completes each sentence.

11. (Do, Does) anybody want to make some popcorn?
12. Nobody else (know, knows) how to fix the screen door.
13. Each of the children (was, were) allowed to look through the binoculars.
14. It looks like somebody (has, have) tried to open this lock.
15. Everyone (has, have) been looking forward to the concert.

Name: _____ **Date:** _____

Demonstrative pronouns refer to specific nouns.

This is a beautiful shade of green. Is that your favorite color?

The pronouns *this* and *that* refer to singular nouns. The pronouns *these* and *those* are plural. *This* and *these* refer to nouns that are nearby. *That* and *those* refer to nouns that are farther away.

Everyone brought some cookies. **These** are delicious.

Those cookies over there are not so good.

Demonstrative pronouns serve as the subject of verbs. However, *this, that, these,* and *those* can also be used as demonstrative adjectives. When they are used with a noun, they are adjectives.

Demonstrative Adjective: This cookie is crumbly.

Demonstrative Pronoun: This is a crumbly cookie.

Directions: Write the demonstrative pronoun in each sentence.
Underline the noun that the demonstrative pronoun refers to.

1. Are these the brownies Amy made last night? _____

2. Those are delicious cheesecake bars in that pan. _____

3. This is the biggest platter Jorge could find. _____

4. That recipe is pretty easy to make when you're in a hurry. _____

5. This is the best potluck we've had in long time! _____

Directions: Write the pronoun that correctly completes each sentence on the line.

6. (This, These) is my neighborhood. _____

7. (These, Those) are Mr. Ruben's rose bushes here. _____

8. (This, That) is the park over there. _____

9. (That, Those) are the kids I often play with. _____

10. (This, That) is my apartment building here. _____

11. (This, These) are the stairs that lead to my floor. _____

12. (This, That) is my best friend's house at the end of the street. _____

13. (That, Those) are my neighbors, the Wheatleys. _____

14. (This, That) is their dog we're playing with now. _____

15. (This, These) is a good place to live. _____

Name: _____   **Date:** _____

Many questions are formed using an interrogative pronoun. The words *what, who, which, whom,* and *whose* can all be used as interrogative pronouns.

What are the titles of their reports?
Who is the author of that book?
Which article was the most helpful?
Whom did the writers interview?
Whose is the best report?

The words *who* and *whom* are easily confused. *Who* serves as the subject of a verb.

Who is reviewing your paper? (*Who* is the subject of the verb *is reviewing*.)

Whom serves as the object of a verb.

Whom did the students talk to?
(The subject of the verb *talk to* is *students*. The object is *whom*.)

It can be easy to confuse *whose* and *who's*. You have learned that *who's* is a contraction for *who is* or *who has*. Remember that pronouns never have apostrophes.

Who's ready to read their report? (*Who's* = who is)
Of all the reports, **whose** was most interesting?
(*Whose* = interrogative pronoun)

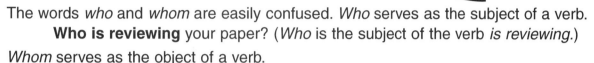

Directions: Underline the interrogative pronoun in each sentence.

1. Which of the two colors did Val choose for the walls?
2. Whose was the oldest fossil?
3. Who remembers the title of last week's story?
4. What is the matter with Hannah?
5. Whom will David meet during his travels?

Directions: Complete each sentence by writing *Who, Whom, Whose,* or *Who's* on the line.

6. _____ is responsible for this mess?
7. _____ might I ask about this problem?
8. _____ going to help me put away the groceries?
9. _____ is the best candidate for the job?
10. _____ should Lisa call to fix the computer?
11. Of all the pies, _____ deserves the blue ribbon?
12. _____ did Amy invite to the recital?
13. _____ ate all the crackers?
14. _____ in charge of cleaning up after the festival?
15. _____ will you babysit tonight?

Name: _____   **Date:** _____

Action verbs show action. They tell what a subject does.

> Graham **dropped** his cell phone on the driveway.
> The plastic casing **broke** into pieces.

Linking verbs do not show action. Instead, linking verbs "link" nouns to information about the nouns.

> Graham **felt** bad. The cell phone **was** ruined.

> **COMMON LINKING VERBS**
>
> am, is, are, was, were, will be, be, being, been
> look, feel, taste, smell, seem, appear, become

Some verbs can function as both action verbs and linking verbs. To decide if a verb is functioning as a linking verb or an action verb, substitute a form of the verb "to be" *(am, is, was, were, be, being, been)* for the verb. If the sentence makes sense, most likely the original verb is a linking verb. If the sentence does not make sense, the verb is probably an action verb.

ORIGINAL SENTENCE	WITH "TO BE" SUBSTITUTED	DOES IT MAKE SENSE?
Graham **looked** upset about the phone.	Graham **was** upset about the phone	Yes: *looked* is a linking verb here.
Graham **looked** at the cell phone and sighed.	Graham **was** at the cell phone and sighed.	No: *looked* is an action verb here.

Directions: Identify each underlined verb as active or linking by writing *A* for active or *L* for linking on the line that follows each one.

Good Vibrations

Kids <u>can be</u> ____ very inventive. Unlike today, when many kids <u>own</u> ____ their own cell phones, kids of yesteryear <u>constructed</u> ____ their own phones—string telephones. A string telephone <u>consists</u> ____ of two tin cans connected by a long piece of string. String telephones actually <u>work</u> ____. Why? Because the speaker's voice <u>produces</u> ____ sound vibrations that <u>resonate</u> ____ or echo, inside the tin can. The vibrations then <u>travel</u> ____ along the string to the tin can at the other end. The string <u>must be</u> ____ very tight so that it <u>will vibrate</u> ____. If the string <u>is</u> ____ too loose, the vibrations will <u>grow</u> ____ weaker and then <u>die</u> ____. When the vibrations <u>reach</u> ____ the second tin can, they <u>cause</u> ____ the can and the air molecules inside it to vibrate. The vibrations are then picked up by your ear and you <u>hear</u> ____ your friend's voice. You may <u>look</u> ____ funny using a tin can phone and the sound <u>isn't</u> ____ perfect, but callers <u>get</u> ____ unlimited minutes year round!

Name: _____   Date: _____

You have learned that a direct object is a word that receives the action of a verb. It answers the question *What?* or *Whom?* about the verb. Some verbs must always have a direct object. These verbs are called **transitive verbs**. A transitive verb is one that directs its action toward a direct object.

> Joy lifts <u>weights</u>.

A verb that does not have a direct object is an **intransitive verb**. In addition, linking verbs are always intransitive.

> The baby cried. (No direct object)
> Jack is a good writer. (Linking verb; no direct object)

Some verbs can be either transitive or intransitive, depending on how they are used.

Transitive	**Intransitive**
Claire closed her eyes.	The store closed.

Directions: What kind of verb is the underlined verb in each sentence? Write *Transitive* or *Intransitive* on the line.

1. Mr. Patterson <u>hums</u> constantly. _____

2. David <u>fished</u> for three hours yesterday. _____

3. Ms. Hanover <u>scheduled</u> the meeting for 3:00. _____

4. Ricardo <u>saw</u> the car roll into the ditch. _____

5. Spring <u>arrived</u> early this year. _____

6. Jamie and Wilson <u>laughed</u> for hours after the movie. _____

7. Stacy <u>watched</u> carefully as the chemicals fizzled in the beaker. _____

8. Amanda <u>wrapped</u> the dishes in old newspaper. _____

9. The cat <u>chased</u> the flashlight beam across the floor. _____

10. The new museum <u>opens</u> in three weeks. _____

11. Yasmine <u>heard</u> a strange noise coming from the basement. _____

12. The balloon man <u>fascinated</u> the toddlers. _____

13. The passing car <u>splashed</u> mud on my new pants. _____

14. The band <u>practices</u> every Tuesday night until 9:00. _____

15. Iris <u>walked</u> with Sasha to the corner store. _____

16. The old paint <u>came</u> off in a single layer. _____

17. Elliot <u>played</u> a harmless trick on his friend Joe. _____

18. Little Walter still <u>has</u> trouble with tying his shoes. _____

Name: _____ **Date:** _____

Sometimes the verb in a sentence is made up of two parts: one or more **helping verbs** followed by a **main verb**. Together, they are called a verb phrase. The main verb is the most important verb. It shows the action of the subject. The helping verb or verbs do not show action.

SENTENCE	HELPING VERBS	MAIN VERB
Eldrick **is** a good golfer.	–	is
Has he **been practicing** his golf swing every day?	has, been	practicing
Eldrick **has** not always **been** a good golfer.	has	been
Perhaps he **will** someday **win** tournaments.	will	win

Notice that the helping verb may be separated from the main verb by the subject or other words. Also, the word *not* is not considered part of the verb phrase.

COMMON HELPING VERBS

am	were	do	should	may	have
is	be	does	would	can	has
are	being	did	might	shall	had
was	been	could	must	will	

Directions: In the passage below, underline the main verbs once and the helping verbs twice.

Tiger Woods, Golf Superstar

Tiger Woods was born Eldrick Woods on December 30, 1975. His career as a golfer began at a very early age. At the age of 2, he played golf with comedian and golfer Bob Hope on national television. At the age of 3, he was famous in the golf world for shooting 48 on 9 holes, a score many adults would be proud of. By the time he was 15, he had won the Optimist International Junior Tournament 6 times. At 16, he played in the Nissan Los Angeles Open, and by the time he was 17, he had participated in 3 Professional Golfers' Association (PGA) events. By the end of 1994, he had won the Western Amateur Championship and had represented the United States in the World Amateur Team Championships in France. Even as an amateur, Tiger was making and breaking records, and the magazine *Sports Illustrated* chose him as their 1996 Sportsman of the Year. Since then, he has been named Male Athlete of the Year by the Associated Press, ESPY Male Athlete of the Year , and PGA Tour Player of the Year. But no matter what people call him, no name can sum him up better than "Tiger."

Name: _____   Date: _____

Tense tells readers and listeners when an action takes place. **Present tense** verbs are used for action that is taking place now or that is always true.

> Hannah **wants** to go outside. (The action is occurring now.)
>
> Water **freezes** at 32 degrees Fahrenheit. (This is always true.)

Past tense verbs show that the action has already happened.

> Mr. Ahmad **played** the school song at the assembly.

Future tense verbs describe an action that will happen later. The future tense consists of a main verb and the helping verb *will* or *shall*.

> The bell **will ring** in three minutes.

Directions: Write the appropriate form of the verb in parentheses.

1. Last night we _____ Dad's birthday. (celebrate)

2. The first Earth Day _____ in 1970. (occur)

3. The planets _____ around the Sun. (revolve)

4. Do you think everyone _____ the party tomorrow night? (enjoy)

5. Plants _____ sunshine and water to live. (require)

6. Nina _____ her answers before she handed her quiz in. (check)

7. I _____ the video as soon as everyone sits down. (start)

8. In the past, people _____ mainly by foot or by horseback. (travel)

9. Right now, most people _____ around by car or bus. (get)

10. In the future, perhaps we _____ around with mini jet-packs. (zoom)

Directions: For each verb, write a sentence in the tense indicated.

11. (grow—Present) _____

_____

12. (yawn—Past) _____

_____

13. (accompany—Future) _____

_____

14. (confess—Past) _____

_____

15. (oppose—Present) _____

_____

Name: _____ **Date:** _____

A present tense verb must agree in number with the subject. Follow these rules for forming present tense verbs for singular subjects.

RULES FOR FORMING PRESENT TENSE VERBS		
Most verbs	add –s	sleep–She sleeps.
Verbs that end in –s, –sh, –ch, –z, or –x	add –es	mix–He mixes.
Verbs that end in a consonant + y	change the y to i and add –es	hurry–She hurries.

Past tense verbs show actions that have already happened. Follow these rules for forming past tense verbs.

RULES FOR FORMING PAST TENSE VERBS		
Most verbs	add –ed	talk–talked
Verbs that end in –e	drop the –e and add –ed	change–changed
Verbs that end in a consonant + y	change the y to i and add –ed	study–studied
Verbs that end with one vowel followed by one consonant	double the consonant and add –ed	hop–hopped

Directions: Write the past tense form of each verb.

1. lace _____

2. purchase _____

3. snatch _____

4. skip _____

5. revise _____

6. occupy _____

7. enjoy _____

8. buckle _____

9. succeed _____

10. marry _____

Directions: If the sentence is in the past tense, rewrite it in the present tense. If it is in the present tense, rewrite it in the past tense.

11. The hummingbird sipped delicately at the feeder.

_____

12. The cat watches the giant beetle intently.

_____

13. Xavier never varied his weekend routine.

_____

14. The engine propels the rocket into the air.

_____

Name: _____ **Date:** _____

Present tense verbs must agree in number with the subject of the sentence. The subject pronouns *I, he, she,* and *it* take singular verbs. The subject pronoun *they* is plural and requires a plural verb. The subject pronoun *you* can be either singular or plural. When *you* replaces a singular subject, it requires a singular verb. When *you* replaces a plural subject, it requires a plural verb.

Wilson Rawls is a wonderful author.   **He** is a wonderful author. (singular verb)
His **stories** take place in Oklahoma.   **They** take place in Oklahoma. (plural verb)

Directions: Underline the correct form of each verb for the subject pronouns in the book review below.

What happens when a boy, a dog, and a band of monkeys meet in the river bottoms of Oklahoma's Ozark Mountains? Plenty! *Summer of the Monkeys* by Wilson Rawls is a humorous and heartwarming book. It (tells/tell) the story of Jay Berry Lee and his dog Rowdy, who spend a summer trying to capture 29 monkeys that have escaped from a traveling circus. Jay Berry is a happy 14-year-old boy whose life could be happier, he believes, if he only had a pony and a .22 rifle. He (sees/see) his chance to get both when a reward is offered for the capture of a band of circus monkeys. Jay Berry and Rowdy are sure they (is/are) up to the task. After all, they

(has/have) Jay Berry's grandfather to advise them. But taking on a band of trained monkeys is more than they (bargains/bargain) for. It (doesn't/don't) take long for them to learn that monkeys can bite—hard!—and that they (is/are) very smart! So smart, in fact, that they (steals/steal) Jay Berry's traps *after* enjoying the apples they (is/are) baited with. Will Grandpa come up with a successful plan to catch the clever monkeys? Will Jay Berry get his pony and rifle? Find out for yourself by reading *Summer of the Monkeys.* It (is/are) a good read!

Name: _____   **Date:** _____

MORE SUBJECT VERB AGREEMENT

When the subject of a sentence is easy to find, it's usually easy to make it agree with the verb. But subjects are not always obvious. Look at this example.

This batch of cookies is ready.

In this sentence, the plural noun *cookies* is the noun closest to the verb *is*. However, *of cookies* is a prepositional phrase, and the subject of a sentence is never found in a prepositional phrase. *Batch* is the subject of the sentence. Since *batch* is singular, it requires the singular verb *is*. Remember, when a phrase or clause falls between the subject and the verb, the verb must still agree with the subject.

The **woman** who was pictured in the newspaper shaking hands with the two ambassadors **happens** to be our state senator.

Directions: Circle the simple subject of each sentence. The verb has been underlined for you.

1. The man Tom saw yesterday at the gas station <u>works</u> at the grocery store.

2. Some of the pudding you made <u>has dripped</u> onto the counter.

3. The plant with the heart-shaped leaves <u>needs</u> water.

4. The mold growing on the inside of the refrigerator <u>should be cleaned</u> off.

5. The silver, two-door car that Deborah drives <u>gets</u> good gas mileage.

Directions: Underline the subject of each sentence and the correct form of the verb.

6. One of those students (needs/need) a new lunch ticket.

7. This bushel of apples (was/were) picked yesterday.

8. The head counselor of the summer camp (teach/teaches) art.

9. Three pages of the book I bought yesterday at Gordon's (is/are) missing.

10. One of the plates in that set (has/have) a chip off the rim.

11. The students in the Spanish Club (is/are) holding a bake sale.

12. The mayor, as well as his two aides, (attends/attend) the monthly meeting.

13. The team, accompanied by the coaches, (boards/board) the bus at noon.

14. All apples except the Granny Smiths (costs/cost) a dollar a pound.

15. The enormous swarm of locusts (eat/eats) every green thing in its path.

Name: _____   **Date:** _____

62   *Language Arts Skills & Strategies, Level 7* • Saddleback Publishing, Inc. ©2005 • 3 Watson, Irvine, CA 92618 • Phone (888) 735-2225 • www.sdlback.com

An **irregular verb** is a verb that does not take *–ed* in the past tense. Irregular verbs have special past tense spellings that must be remembered.

PRESENT	PAST	PAST PARTICIPLE
am, is, are	was, were	(has, have, had) been
have, has	had	(has, have, had) had
do, does	did	(has, have, had) done
come, comes	came	(has, have, had) come
fight, fights	fought	(has, have, had) fought
put, puts	put	(has, have, had) put
know, knows	knew	(has, have, had) known
blow, blows	blew	(has, have, had) blown
throw, throws	threw	(has, have, had) thrown
draw, draws	drew	(has, have, had) drawn

Directions: Write the correct past tense form of the verb in parentheses on the line.

1. Kylie _____ pretty well on her Spanish test yesterday. (do)

2. DeWayne folded the note and _____ it in his back pocket. (put)

3. That sign has _____ over three times already today. (blow)

4. The pitcher has _____ the first pitch of the game already. (throw)

5. Lori _____ cereal for breakfast. (have)

6. Before Sherman _____ to our neighborhood, life was dull. (come)

7. Without a doubt, this has _____ the best day of my life! (be)

8. Those neighbors have _____ about the loud music before. (fight)

9. Lionel _____ a fit when his favorite team lost. (throw)

10. Amy knew that Patrick had _____ to say goodbye. (come)

11. All the actors _____ a great job with the production. (do)

12. Paul and Eric have _____ each other since kindergarten. (know)

13. Dan _____ a single, clear note on his trumpet. (blow)

14. This author's ideas have _____ a big effect on me. (have)

15. The jugglers _____ a big crowd at the festival. (draw)

Name: _____ **Date:** _____

The following table lists more verbs that have irregular past tense forms.

PRESENT	PAST	PAST PARTICIPLE
tear, tears	tore	(has, have, had) torn
wear, wears	wore	(has, have, had) worn
break, breaks	broke	(has, have, had) broken
buy, buys	bought	(has, have, had) bought
sell, sells	sold	(has, have, had) sold
eat, eats	ate	(has, have, had) eaten
drink, drinks	drank	(has, have, had) drunk
give, gives	gave	(has, have, had) given
hold, holds	held	(has, have, had) held
ride, rides	rode	(has, have, had) ridden

Directions: Write the correct past tense form of the verb in parentheses on the line.

1. The paper had _____ neatly at the fold line. (tear)

2. Sam _____ a subscription to a weekly news magazine. (buy)

3. The glue has _____ that chair leg in place for a long time, but I think it will break again soon. (hold)

4. All the dancers _____ red sashes over their white dresses. (wear)

5. When Nick came in from playing, he found that his brothers had _____ all the lemonade. (drink)

6. Mr. Lemmon has _____ $200 to that charity so far this year. (give)

7. Grant's jacket pocket _____ when it got caught on the doorknob. (tear)

8. Lacey's car _____ down in the middle of the intersection. (break)

9. Jessie didn't like the new slippers her mother had _____ for her. (buy)

10. Ivan _____ his bike all the way to the mall yesterday. (ride)

11. Mrs. Winston felt her husband had _____ their car for too little. (sell)

12. The hungry campers _____ every last bit of the cornbread and chili. (eat)

13. Mrs. Knight has _____ her hair the same way for thirty years. (wear)

14. The Taylors _____ the wedding reception in their lovely backyard. (hold)

15. The persuasive salesman _____ Bob five sets of steak knives. (sell)

Name: _____   **Date:** _____

Perfect tenses consist of two parts: the helping verb *has, have,* or *had* and the past participle of the main verb. The three perfect tenses are present perfect, past perfect, and future perfect.

TENSE	HOW TO FORM IT	EXAMPLE
Present Perfect Tense: used to express actions that happened at an unspecified time in the past. The action might still be happening.	has/have + past participle	We have watched this movie before.
Past Perfect Tense: used to express actions that happened before a certain time in the past	had + past participle	I had opened the box before I noticed the warning label.
Future Perfect Tense: used to express action that will be completed before another event in the future.	will + have + past participle	We will have finished our report by the end of the week.

Directions: What tense is the underlined verb in each sentence? Write *Present Perfect, Past Perfect,* or *Future Perfect* on the line.

1. Mira <u>will have finished</u> the book by the end of the day. _____

2. Rose <u>has bungled</u> her way through that song eight times. _____

3. Caroline <u>had hiked</u> three miles by noon. _____

4. Trent <u>had participated</u> in three marathons by age 17. _____

5. Bats <u>have invaded</u> many of these abandoned warehouses. _____

Directions: Write the correct form of the verb *have* that goes with the tense indicated in parentheses.

6. Jamie _____ purchased a new game. (present perfect)

7. That club _____ hosted several guest speakers this year. (present perfect)

8. Jeb _____ watched three sitcoms before he went to bed. (past perfect)

9. William _____ distributed the team uniforms by now. (future perfect)

10. Gabe _____ earned a lot of money at the farmer's market. (present perfect)

Name: _____   **Date:** _____

Perfect tenses consist of two parts: the helping verb *has, have,* or *had* and the past participle of the main verb.

TENSE	HOW TO FORM IT	EXAMPLE
Present Perfect Tense	has/have + past participle	She has tried to reach you.
Past Perfect Tense	had + past participle	He had discovered a new medicine.
Future Perfect Tense	will + have + past participle	The weather will have improved by next week.

Directions: Complete the chart by writing the perfect tense forms of each verb in the appropriate columns. The first row has been done for you.

VERB	PRESENT PERFECT	PAST PERFECT	FUTURE PERFECT
toss	he has tossed	had tossed	will have tossed
1. prepare	I _____	_____	_____
2. gather	we _____	_____	_____
3. trap	they _____	_____	_____
4. enjoy	it _____	_____	_____
5. plant	you _____	_____	_____

Directions: Rewrite each sentence, changing the underlined verb to the tense shown in parentheses.

6. Henry <u>decides</u> he didn't like asparagus even before he tried it. (past perfect)

_____

7. Candle wax <u>drips</u> all over the new tablecloth. (present perfect)

_____

8. It <u>stops</u> snowing by the time Chris gets his boots on. (future perfect)

_____

9. Seeing your smiling face <u>lifts</u> my spirits. (present perfect)

_____

10. We rushed out to see the rainbow, but it <u>disappears</u> already. (past perfect)

_____

Name: _____ **Date:** _____

As you have learned, a transitive verb is a verb that directs its action towards a direct object. Sentences with transitive verbs can usually be written in either the active voice or the passive voice. In the active voice, the subject of the sentence is the "doer" of the verb action. The action of the verb is then directed towards the direct object.

> Active Voice: Jackson **ate** four doughnuts this morning. (*Jackson* is the "doer" of the action *ate.* The direct object *doughnuts* receives the action of the verb.)

In the passive voice, the direct object (doughnuts) becomes the subject, and the "doer" becomes the receiver of the verb.

> Passive Voice: Four doughnuts **were eaten** by Jackson this morning. (*Jackson* is still the "doer," but he is not the subject of the sentence.)

Directions: In what voice is each sentence written? Write *Active* or *Passive* on the line.

1. The children write stories. _____

2. Stories are written by the children. _____

3. Most students made few mistakes. _____

4. Few mistakes were made by most students. _____

5. The bus will be driven by Ms. Sampson. _____

6. Ms. Sampson will drive the bus. _____

7. The peaceful afternoon is shattered by the sirens. _____

8. The sirens and clanging bells shatter the peaceful afternoon. _____

9. The books should be arranged in alphabetical order. _____

10. They should arrange the books in alphabetical order. _____

Directions: These sentences are in the passive voice. Read each one and underline the verb. Circle the "doer" of the verb's action. Then write the active form of the verb on the line. One example has been done for you.

> **EXAMPLE:** Matt and David <u>were given</u> the blue ribbon by the (judge.) *gave* ___

11. Kathy was scolded by her aunt. _____

12. The cabin is surrounded by pine trees. _____

13. Soon the field will be covered by the floodwaters. _____

14. The teachers are pleased by your improvement. _____

15. We were saddened by the news. _____

Name: _____   **Date:** _____

In active voice, the "doer" is the subject. In passive voice, the object is the subject.

ACTIVE VOICE	PASSIVE VOICE
Marsha will care for the plants.	The plants will be cared for by Marsha.
The students planned the surprise.	The surprise was planned by the students.
The question baffles Peter.	Peter is baffled by the question.
Rory can solve the mystery.	The mystery can be solved by Rory.

Directions: These sentences are in the passive voice. Rewrite them in the active voice.

1. The movie was seen by all the students.

   _____

2. A wonderful party will be given by the parents.

   _____

3. The children's toys were taken away by the mean babysitter.

   _____

4. This story can be understood by small children.

   _____

5. The track star's record was shattered by the unknown runner.

   _____

Directions: These sentences are in the active voice. Rewrite them in the passive voice.

6. The baseball broke the window.

   _____

7. The author will read the stories.

   _____

8. The police will interview all the suspects.

   _____

9. Fifty students can attend the scientist's lecture.

   _____

10. A panel of judges reviews each contestant's project.

   _____

Name: _____   **Date:** _____

Some verbs are easily confused. *Lay, raise,* and *set* are very often transitive verbs. They must be followed by direct objects. *Lie, rise,* and *sit* are nearly always intransitive.

PRESENT	PAST	WITH *HAS, HAVE* OR *HAD*
lay, lays	laid	(has, have, had) lain
lie, lies	lay	(has, have, had) laid
raise, raises	raised	(has, have, had) raised
rise, rises	rose	(has, have, had) risen
set, sets	set	(has, have, had) set
sit, sits	sat	(has, have, had) sat

VERB	MEANING	EXAMPLE
lay	to put or place something	Salem lays the book down.
lie	to rest or recline	Salem lies on the couch.
raise	to move something up, to increase, or to grow something	Susanne raises her hand.
rise	To move from a lower to higher position	The sun rises in the east.
set	to put or place something	Oscar sets the alarm for 6:00.
sit	to rest in a seated position	Oscar sits in the front row.

Directions: Underline the correct verb in parentheses.

1. Miranda is (setting/sitting) on the most comfortable chair in the room.

2. Miranda is (setting/sitting) her book bag on the chair.

3. The dogs (lie/lay) in their kennel.

4. The dogs (lie/lay) their rawhide bones next to them in the kennel.

5. That milk has been (setting/sitting) out for hours.

6. That rug does not (lay/lie) flat on the floor.

7. Amelia's spirits (raised/rose) when she read the letter from Grandma.

8. Malcolm (sat/set) lost in thought for hours, simply gazing out the window.

9. Everyone should know that hot air (raises/rises).

10. The dress was (lain/laid) out on the bed, ready to be put on.

11. When my dad was a boy, his family (raised/rose) rabbits.

12. If you are tired, (lay/lie) your head on the desk and rest your eyes.

An infinitive is a verb form that can serve many functions in a sentence. An infinitive is the basic form of the verb, usually beginning with the word *to.* An infinitive phrase consists of an infinitive plus any words that go with it.

I like **to sleep** late on Saturday mornings.
I like **to sleep late on Saturday mornings**.

A gerund is a verb form ending in *–ing* that functions as a noun.
A gerund phrase is a gerund plus any words that go with it.

Gerund: **Sailing** is an excellent pastime.
Gerund Phrase: You'll need rubber gloves for **scrubbing the garbage can**.

Directions: Underline the infinitive or infinitive phrase in each sentence.

1. That little café is the best place to eat pancakes.
2. Mr. Massey is not someone to put off decisions.
3. Hilary jogged to keep herself fit.
4. The squirrel tried to bury the nut in the hard clay ground.
5. To fly commercial airliners has always been Wayne's goal.
6. The wind ruined the balloonist's attempt to take off this morning.
7. Cami read that book to learn more about Hopi Indians.
8. The Spanish Club wanted to raise $100 for their fieldtrip.
9. Oretha went to college to study engineering.
10. Oscar asked his mother to take him to the mall.

Directions: Provide a gerund that makes sense for each sentence.

11. _____ is a fun thing to do in the summer.
12. _____ really scares me.
13. _____ is a good way to pass the time on a rainy day.
14. _____ takes a lot of practice.
15. _____ is only for daredevils.
16. I think _____ would be an interesting career.
17. I can only stand _____ for so long.
18. _____ is my all-time favorite thing to do.
19. I wish I were better at _____.
20. _____ is never a good thing to do.

Name: _____ **Date:** _____

Adjectives are words that modify, or describe, nouns, or pronouns.
Adjectives can tell *what kind, how many,* or *which one.*
Adjectives usually come before the word they modify.

Most of **these French** fries are **cold**.

Let's ask **that friendly** waiter for **some hot** ones.

WHAT KIND	HOW MANY	WHICH
French, cold, friendly, hot, red, baked, squishy	most, some, three, several, all, every, many	these, that, the, either, your, this, those

A proper adjective is one that is formed from a proper noun. Like a proper noun, proper adjectives are capitalized.

German shepherd   Irish stew   Egyptian pyramids

A, an, and *the* are special adjectives called **articles**. The demonstrative adjectives *this, that, these,* and *those* tell *which one* or *which ones.*

Directions: Circle each adjective, article, and demonstrative adjective in the following sentences. Then draw an arrow to the noun or pronoun each one modifies.

EXAMPLE: That red car needs a new engine.

1. This recipe calls for ripe tomatoes, one onion, and Greek olives.

2. The stores in this mall have been open for six weeks.

3. Reggie made an interesting discovery when he opened the wooden crate.

4. The hot sand felt warm and soothing under Chris's feet.

5. Oliver loves Belgian waffles with cream and fresh strawberries.

6. The library is empty on this sunny afternoon.

7. The shiny surface of the table gleamed in the soft candlelight.

8. Many people dislike moving to a new city, but I like it.

9. It has been eight years since I saw my good friend Hank.

10. Tanya saw two tiny lights flickering in the darkness.

Name: _____   **Date:** _____

Adjectives can be used to compare people, places, or things. There are different degrees of comparison. The positive degree simply describes one person, place, or thing. The comparative degree, which compares two nouns, is formed by adding –er to most adjectives. Add –est to most adjectives to form the superlative degree, which compares three or more nouns.

Positive   **Comparative**   **Superlative**
My stereo is **loud**.   Yours is **louder**.   DeWayne's is **loudest**.

This table shows how to form adjectives that compare.

If the adjective ends in –e, drop the –e and add the ending.	nice–nicer–nicest
If the adjective ends with a consonant + y, change the y to i and add the ending.	easy–easier–easiest
If the adjective ends with one vowel followed by one consonant, double the consonant and add the ending.	red–redder–reddest
For most adjectives that have two syllables and all adjectives with three or more syllables, use more or most.	careful–more careful–most careful amazing–more amazing–most amazing

Directions: Write the comparative and superlative forms of each adjective.

1. heavy, _____, _____
2. new, _____, _____
3. talented, _____, _____
4. dull, _____, _____
5. large, _____, _____

6. incredible _____, _____
7. sad, _____, _____
8. soft, _____, _____
9. helpful, _____, _____
10. fancy, _____, _____

Directions: Underline the correct form of the adjective in parentheses.

11. Heavy fabrics are usually (warmer, warmest) than light ones.

12. Of all the girls here, Gretchen is the (older, oldest).

13. This is the (huger, hugest) fish Sam has ever caught.

14. The water in the pool is (cooler, coolest) than the water in the lake.

15. Is it my imagination, or is George (taller, tallest) than he was last week?

Name: _____   **Date:** _____

Some adjectives are irregular. Their comparative and superlative degrees are not formed by adding *–er* or *–est.*

POSITIVE	COMPARATIVE	SUPERLATIVE
good	better	best
bad	worse	worst
well (healthy)	better	best
little (amount)	less	least
much, many	more	most

The word *well* can be an adverb or an adjective. When *well* is used as an adjective, it means *healthy.* As an adverb, it means *in a good or proper way.*

Adjective: I was sick yesterday, but now I am well. (*well* modifies *I*)
Adverb: April plays the piano well. (*well* modifies *plays*)

Directions: Complete each sentence by writing the positive, comparative, or superlative form of the adjective in parentheses.

1. There are _____ people at the meeting tonight than at the last meeting. (many)

2. There is _____ reason to worry about meteors hitting Earth. (little)

3. Of these plants, the cactus requires the _____ water. (little)

4. It doesn't take _____ money to buy a pen. (much)

5. The TV reception in this area is very _____. (bad)

6. Xavier is the _____ catcher on our team this season. (good)

7. The results of the experiment showed that students who stayed up late get _____ scores than those who slept more. (bad)

8. Hannah has the flu; I hope she gets _____ soon. (well)

9. Emmanuel's first cd was _____ than his first. (good)

10. The cut on my foot is _____ than it was yesterday. (well)

11. The spaghetti Ralph made is really _____. (good)

12. When Nina skips breakfast, she has _____ energy than usual. (little)

13. _____ people thought that movie was hilarious, but I didn't. (many)

14. Barry says KXOK is the _____ radio station around. (bad)

15. Elsie needs a score of _____ than 9.4 to get the gold medal. (much)

Name: _____   **Date:** _____

Adverbs usually modify verbs, but they can also modify adjectives and other adverbs. Adverbs tell *how, when, where,* or *to what extent.*

Adverbs modify verbs.
Teresa **quickly** answered the teacher's first question. (*quickly* modifies *answered*)
Albert **hesitantly** offered an answer to the second question.
     (*hesitantly* modifies *offered*)

Adverbs modify adjectives.
Teresa was **very** proud. (*very* modifies *proud*)
Albert was **slightly** embarrassed. (*slightly* modifies *embarrassed*)

Adverbs modify other adverbs.
The teacher knew **quite** quickly who had done the assignment.
     (*quite* modifies *quickly*)

Directions: Underline the adverb in each sentence.

1. Albert did his homework quickly.

2. Teresa eagerly answered every question.

3. Teresa always did her homework.

4. The teacher never accepts excuses.

5. The teacher gave an extremely difficult assignment.

Directions: Circle each adverb and draw an arrow to the word it modifies.
Note: some of the sentences have more than one adverb.

6. The dog suddenly snapped at the veterinarian.

7. Liz never expected to leave Tallahassee, but her mother got a job in New York.

8. The extremely loud music made the pictures on the wall vibrate.

9. That radio station only plays oldies.

10. The railroad signals were malfunctioning, but luckily no accidents occurred.

11. The students were very disappointed because the field trip had been cancelled unexpectedly.

12. Eduardo impatiently waited in line for tickets.

13. Clarice is barely tall enough to ride that roller coaster.

14. The team tried really hard to win the game but failed miserably.

15. The tornado hit the rural area and seriously damaged some farm buildings.

Name: _____   **Date:** _____

Adverbs can be used to compare actions. Like adjectives, adverbs have positive, comparative, and superlative degrees. Add *–er* to most short adverbs to form the comparative. Add *–est* to form the superlative, which compares three or more actions. For most adverbs of two or more syllables and adverbs that end in *–ly,* use *more* or *most* to compare.

soon, sooner, soonest   rapidly, more rapidly, most rapidly

Some adverbs have irregular comparative forms:

POSITIVE	COMPARATIVE	SUPERLATIVE
well (in a good manner)	better	best
badly	worse	worst
far	farther	farthest
little (degree)	less	least
much (degree)	more	most

Directions: Write the form of the comparative and superlative form of each adverb.

1. late, _____, _____

2. happily, _____, _____

3. fast, _____, _____

4. early, _____, _____

5. carefully, _____, _____

6. little, _____, _____

7. hard, _____, _____

8. far, _____, _____

9. nervously, _____, _____

10. badly, _____, _____

Directions: The underlined phrase in each sentence contains an error. Rewrite each sentence correctly.

11. The cat yowled <u>more louder than</u> any other cat in the alley.

_____

12. The home team performed <u>less skillfuller than</u> the visiting team.

_____

13. My sister plays the tuba <u>worser than</u> I do.

_____

14. That mountain stands <u>highest than</u> any peak in the range.

_____

15. We traveled <u>more far</u> this summer than we have before.

_____

Name: _____   **Date:** _____

Language Arts Skills & Strategies, Level 7 • Saddleback Publishing, Inc. ©2005 • 3 Watson, Irvine, CA 92618 • Phone (888) 735-2225 • www.sdlback.com   75

Always use an adjective to modify a noun or pronoun. Use adverbs to modify verbs.

Adjective	**Adverb**
John is **nervous** before his performance.	He **taps** his foot **nervously**.

Certain adjectives and adverbs are easy to confuse. It is easy to confuse *good* with *well* and *bad* with *badly. Good* and *bad* are adjectives that modify nouns. Use *good* and *bad* before a noun or after a linking verb. You can also use *well* as an adjective meaning "healthy."

It's a **good day** for biking.	The **breeze** feels **good**.

Use *well* and *badly* to modify verbs.

The engine **performs well**.	The interview **went badly**.

Directions: Underline the word that correctly completes each sentence.

1. The garden looks (beautiful, beautifully) this week.

2. You have time to take a (quick, quickly) shower before school.

3. David was (good, well) yesterday, but today he has the sniffles and a cough.

4. The woman with the red hat looked (familiar, familiarly) to me.

5. The reed mat felt (rough, roughly) under Jana's bare feet.

6. Tara's new cell phone doesn't work very (good, well).

7. Be careful; that suitcase is (real, really) heavy.

8. This recipe sounds (good, well).

9. Fred did (bad, badly) at rehearsal, but he'll be fine tonight.

10. That old washing machine still works (great, well).

11. Bloodhounds are (real, really) good at following a scent.

12. The plane will be taking off (immediate, immediately).

13. Jason thought the show was pretty (good, well).

14. We all felt (bad, badly) that you couldn't come to the park with us.

15. What is the (real, really) reason that Gary stayed home from practice?

Name: _____   **Date:** _____

Placing an adverb in the wrong place in a sentence can confuse a reader. Adverbs that modify adjectives and adverbs should be placed next to the words they modify.

The caramel sauce will be **perfectly smooth** and delicious on ice cream. (*perfectly* modifies the adjective *smooth*)

Adverbs that modify verbs may often be placed in various locations in a sentence. You must make certain, however, that the sentence expresses what you want it to say. Look at how the placement of the modifier "only" can affect meaning in the following sentences.

Last year **only**, I was a member of our school's chess team. (Meaning: I was on the team in no other year.)

Last year, **only** I was a member of our school's chess team. (Meaning: There was no other member on the team.)

Directions: Rewrite the following sentences so that the boldfaced word is modified by the adverb. The first one is done for you.

1. Rob **wants** to really get a good score on the test.
   Rob really wants to get a good score on the test.

2. Campers only will need to bring **one** dollar for lunch.
   _____

3. The speaker nearly devoted **an entire** hour to his thoughts on recycling.
   _____

4. That guy exactly looks **like** my cousin.
   _____

5. After a year of French, I could **understand** what Mr. Laurent said easily.
   _____

6. I **heard** Ms. Quinn say definitely she might give us a surprise quiz.
   _____

Directions: For each sentence, draw an arrow to show where you should insert the word *only* to give the sentence the meaning indicated in parentheses.

7. Next week, I can be the secretary of the French Club. (Meaning: There is no other person who can serve as secretary next week.)

8. Next week, I can be the secretary of the French Club. (Meaning: There is just one French Club.)

Directions: Underline the correct adjective or adverb in each pair of words in parentheses.

1. The plant grew so (quick, quickly) that I had to get a bigger pot for it.

2. The growth rate of this plant, however, is quite (slow, slowly).

3. The (russian, Russian) folkdancers performed at (the, these) festival.

4. The cheese biscuits taste (good, well) with soup.

5. Diamonds and gold are (real, really) expensive.

6. Eagles and other birds of prey have (extreme, extremely) sharp eyesight.

7. Your oral report will go (smoother, more smoothly) if you practice it several times.

8. Those hills are (more far, farther) away than they appear.

9. The Rolands are our (most distant, distantest) neighbors.

10. Do you believe that the customers who complain (more, most) of all get the best service?

Directions: Write the word that is modified by the underlined word.

11. The principal was <u>very</u> understanding of the problem. _____

12. She was quite <u>willing</u> to offer suggestions. _____

13. Jackie sleeps <u>quite</u> peacefully in spite of the storm. _____

14. The roast beef was <u>perfectly</u> cooked. _____

15. The old-fashioned lawn mower worked surprisingly <u>well</u>. _____

Directions: Complete each sentence by writing the correct form of the adjective or adverb in parentheses.

16. Haley ran the _____ of any contestant that day. (fast)

17. Only _____ materials were used to make this house. (fine)

18. Jayla likes this brand of toothpaste _____ than the others. (well).

19. Mrs. Hensley spoke _____ than her opponent. (forcefully)

20. Of all the candidates, Mrs. Hensley is the _____. (experienced)

Name: _____　　**Date:** _____

Prepositions are words that show the relationship between a noun or pronoun and another word in a sentence. The noun or pronoun that follows a preposition is called the object of the preposition. A preposition may have a compound preposition.

prep.   obj.   obj.

The squirrel buried an acorn in a pile **of** dried **leaves** and **grass**.

COMMON PREPOSITIONS

about	behind	except	like	through
across	beside	from	of	to
after	between	in	out	under
around	despite	in front of	outside	until
because of	during	inside	over	upon

A **prepositional phrase** is made up of a preposition, the object of the preposition, and all the words that come between them. A prepositional phrase can fall anywhere in a sentence, and a sentence may have more than one prepositional phrase.
<u>Because of the heat</u>, we worried <u>about the runners</u>.

Directions: Underline each prepositional phrase, and then write the preposition and its object on the line.

1. The campers slept beneath the stars, surrounded by pine trees.

   _____

2. Ned tossed his books in his locker and ran to class.

   _____

3. According to this book, the first person to drive across the country was Horatio Jackson.

   _____

4. The twins toddled around the house, dragging their little wagons behind them.

   _____

5. The jalapeño peppers are stuffed with cream cheese, and then a piece of bacon is wrapped around each one.

   _____

Directions: Provide prepositional phrases that make sense for the following sentences.

6. That store sells fabric _____ .

7. Our dogs always buries her bones _____ .

8. Chris had his picture taken _____ .

9. That song was recorded _____ .

10. It was too cold to sit _____ .

Name: _____ **Date:** _____

Prepositional phrases can describe nouns and pronouns. A prepositional phrase that describes a noun or pronoun is called an adjective phrase. Adjective phrases most often tell *which one* or *what kind.*

> The little boy **in the pirate costume** is my neighbor. (tells which *boy*)
> Groups **of children** play outside. (tells what kind of *group*)

A sentence may have more than one adjective phrase. One adjective phrase may follow another directly. The two phrases may both modify the same noun or pronoun.

> I see children <u>from my apartment building</u> <u>in costumes</u>.
> (both adjective phrases modify *children*)

Sometimes, the second adjective phrase modifies the object of the first adjective phrase.

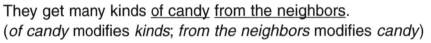

> They get many kinds <u>of candy</u> <u>from the neighbors</u>.
> (*of candy* modifies *kinds*; *from the neighbors* modifies *candy*)

Directions: Underline the adjective phrase or phrases in each sentence. Write the noun or pronoun that each modifies.

1. The band uniforms have blue hats with puffy white plumes.

_____

2. The girl in the red shirt with blue stripes is in my class.

_____

3. The moat of the castle was wide and deep.

_____

4. The nest under the roof of the porch has been there all summer.

_____

5. Everyone except Marcella and me will attend the concert tonight.

_____

6. Bob really likes the actress from that program on TV.

_____

7. Mona made a delicious salad with tomatoes from the farmers' market.

_____

8. The police conducted a search for the stolen bus.

_____

9. The new school board made improvements to the gym and track.

_____

10. Taye got a box of old jewelry from her aunt.

_____

Name: _____   **Date:** _____

When prepositional phrases tell more about verbs, adjectives, or adverbs, they are acting as adverbs and are called adverb phrases. Adverb phrases can tell *how, when, where, why,* or *to what extent.*

This sweater was <u>made</u> **by hand**. (modifies the verb *made;* tells *how*)

The boys were <u>upset</u> **about the news**. (modifies the adjective *upset;* tells *why*)

We rowed <u>far</u> **from the shore**. (modifies the adverb *far;* tells *where*)

We're going to <u>leave</u> **at midnight**. (modifies the verb *leave;* tells *when*)

That store has been <u>closed</u> **for a long time**. (modifies the adjective *closed;* tells *to what extent*)

Like adjective phrases, a sentence can have more than one adverb phrase. The phrases might modify the same word.

Before lunch, the girls went **for a swim**. (both phrases modify the verb *went*)

Directions: Underline the adverb phrase in each sentence. Write the verb, adjective, or adverb that it describes.

1. Gwen accidentally left her purse at the party.

   _____

2. The boys built sand castles on the beach.

   _____

3. The tourists gazed toward Mount Rushmore.

   _____

4. Jayla is crazy about her new baby brother!

   _____

5. Hamilton's button popped off his shirt and landed in his soup.

   _____

6. The teacher plans to go over the quiz results in the last period.

   _____

7. Just look at the mess you've made of your room!

   _____

8. The excitable dog ran around the yard, barking madly at the birds.

   _____

9. Tracy is famous for her hilarious imitations.

   _____

10. The path leads through the woods and past the castle gates.

   _____

Name: _____   **Date:** _____

Sometimes choosing the right preposition can be confusing. The words *between* and *among* have similar meanings. *Beside* and *besides* have similar spellings.

Between and Among   The word *between* refers to two people, places, things, or groups. Use *among* when referring to three or more.

The children ran back and forth between the house and the garden.
They played among the trees all day.

Beside and Besides   The word *beside* means "next to."
Use *besides* when you mean "in addition to."

There is a playhouse beside the garden.
Besides butterflies, the garden is home to birds, insects, and a tortoise.

Directions: Underline the preposition that correctly completes each sentence.

1. The spider sat down (beside, besides) the young woman as she ate her yogurt.

2. There is a big rivalry (between, among) the Hornets and the Bulldogs.

3. (Between, Among) the players on the teams, there is a strong sense of sportsmanship.

4. Who will be at the meeting, (beside, besides) you, me, and the secretary?

5. You must choose (between, among) chocolate and vanilla.

6. There are 31 flavors to choose (between, among) in this shop.

7. There isn't much to do before the party (beside, besides) set out the snacks and put on some good music.

8. Mr. Yang travels 30 miles (between, among) his house and his office every day.

9. Herman isn't interested in much (beside, besides) submarines and computers.

10. The weather forecast is not good for Saturday, but it could change (between, among) now and then.

11. On a table at the flea market, Betty spied a valuable antique lamp (between, among) the old dishes, jars of buttons, and dusty trinkets.

12. A small Turkish carpet lies (beside, besides) the leather armchair.

13. Jack and Tony picked up their rakes, and (between, among) the two of them had the yard cleaned up in no time.

14. The three friends always sit (beside, besides) one another on the bus.

15. The mansion had been locked up tight all night, so the Inspector knew the murderer was (between, among) the people in the house.

Name: _____   **Date:** _____

Prepostional phrases must be placed properly in sentence in order to convey your meaning. Read the following sentences.

A. Lana learned that she was being considered for the award **from her teacher**.

B. Lana learned **from her teacher** that she was being considered for the award.

In sentence A, the reader understands that the award is being given by the teacher; the sentence does not state how Lana learned this. In sentence B, the reader understands that it was the teacher who told Lana that she was being considered; the sentence does not say who is giving the award.

As a general rule, adjective phrases should be placed directly after the words they modify. Adverb phrases should be placed close to the words they modify or at the beginning of the sentence.

Directions: Rewrite each sentence so that the misplaced prepositional phrase is correctly placed and the meaning is clear.

1. The winners were announced on the radio from Lana's class.

   _____

2. Somebody left footprints all over the rug with muddy feet.

   _____

3. Len bought a CD player at a garage sale with a bad speaker.

   _____

4. I saw that the candidate held a huge victory celebration on TV.

   _____

5. Let's watch the show on Channel 12 with my favorite actor.

   _____

6. The French Club held a bake sale to raise money for their trip to France at the mall.

   _____

7. I saw a new book at the bookstore on Main Street by that author.

   _____

8. The library stays open late to accommodate people who work during the day on Monday and Thursday.

   _____

9. Mr. Malik volunteers after breakfast at the animal shelter.

   _____

10. The mother cat carries her kittens every spring out of the barn.

    _____

Name: _____ **Date:** _____

Negatives are words that mean "no" or "not." A double negative occurs when two negatives are used together to express one idea. Do not use double negatives.

Incorrect: Wally did**n't** want **nothing** to eat for breakfast. However, he could**n't hardly** turn down his grandma's pancakes.

Correct: Wally did**n't** want **anything** to eat for breakfast. However, he could **hardly** turn down his grandma's pancakes.

One way to correct a double negative is to substitute a positive word for one of the negatives. The list below shows the most common negatives and their positive equivalents.

no—any   nothing—anything   no one—anyone
none—any   neither—either   never—ever

The words *barely, hardly, scarcely,* and *not* (*n't* in contractions) are also negatives.

Directions: Rewrite the following sentences, correcting the double negative.

1. Morgan didn't bring none of her CD's to the party.

2. "I never worry about nothing," Liam bragged.

3. "Too bad there aren't no tickets left for the concert," Misty said.

4. Mrs. Farrad didn't assignment no homework today.

5. "I can't hardly keep up with all the news today," Mrs. Banks said.

6. "My mom says I never hear nothing she tells me," Russell said.

7. There were hardly no people at the last volleyball game.

8. Beverly was not barely tall enough to ride the log ride at the amusement park.

9. The doctor told Mr. Wonderlin that he shouldn't eat or drink nothing before his surgery.

10. Nobody never wants to play hopscotch with me anymore!

Name: _____   **Date:** _____

A junction is a place where two things, such as roads, meet. A conjunction is a word that brings words or groups of words together. This table lists the most common coordinating conjunctions.

CONJ.	USE OR MEANING	EXAMPLE
for	"because"	There's no use worrying about tomorrow, **for** today is not over yet.
and	Expresses addition.	The dog **and** the cat are due for their vaccinations.
nor	Expresses addition of a negative.	Lane won't play in the game tonight, **nor** will he attend.
but	Expresses contrast.	I like tea, **but** I hate coffee.
or	Presents a choice.	School will start in August **or** September.
yet	"in spite of this"	Fred claims he hates gossip, **yet** he talks behind his friends's backs all the time.
so	"as a result"	The computer lab was open, **so** Brianna started on her research paper.

Directions: Complete each sentence by writing an appropriate coordinating conjunction on the line.

1. I didn't have time to write Uncle Paul a letter, _____ I called him instead.

2. This book brings up strong feelings in people—they either love it _____ hate it.

3. Stacy just loves this band, _____ they never appealed to me.

4. There's no use crying over spilled milk, _____ what's done is done.

5. Start by doing just a few sit-ups per day _____ then gradually increase the number.

6. Neither scrubbing _____ soaking in soapy water removed the stain on Stan's shirt.

7. I haven't seen my old house since I was a toddler, _____ I can still describe it in perfect detail.

8. Is it true that you should wait half an hour after eating before swimming, _____ is that just an old wives' tale?

9. That strange sound we heard last night was nothing _____ a raccoon snuffling around the garbage can.

10. The store was closed by the time we got there, _____ we went home empty handed.

Name: _____ **Date:** _____

Knowing the meaning of word parts can help you learn and understand new words. Prefixes and suffixes all have their own meanings. Knowing the meanings of word roots can also help. The root of a word contains the main meaning of the word, but it cannot stand alone as a word.

WORD ROOT	MEANING	EXAMPLE
dyn, dyna	power	dynamo
ben	good, well	benefit
man	hand	manual
tele	from a distance	television
vita	life	vitality
vid, vis	see	visual

Directions: Write the root of each word. Then write the meaning of each word. You may use a dictionary to help you.

1. telescope _____

2. benefactor _____

3. vitamin _____

4. telephone _____

5. manicure _____

6. dynamite _____

7. revitalize _____

8. vision _____

9. dynasty _____

10. video _____

11. manipulate _____

12. vital _____

13. evident _____

14. telegraph _____

15. dynamic _____

Name: _____   **Date:** _____

A prefix is a letter or a group of letters added to the beginning of a word to make a new word.

reappear—to appear again   **de**frost—to remove frost   **mis**read—to read wrongly

COMMON PREFIXES

com, con, co—with; together
de—reversal; undoing; downward
dis—away, not, reversal
en, em—in; into; to cover or contain

ex—out of; former
in—into; not
mis—badly; wrongly
out—more or better
over—too much
pre—before; ahead of

pro—in favor of
re—again; restore
sub—under; beneath
trans—across
un—opposite of

Directions: Add a prefix from the list to each word. Use a dictionary to make sure the new word is a real word. Then write the meaning of the new word and use it in a sentence.

1. approve   New Word: _____   Meaning: _____
   Sentence: _____

2. honest   New Word: _____   Meaning: _____
   Sentence: _____

3. cover   New Word: _____   Meaning: _____
   Sentence: _____

4. produce   New Word: _____   Meaning: _____
   Sentence: _____

5. place   New Word: _____   Meaning: _____
   Sentence: _____

6. happy   New Word: _____   Meaning: _____
   Sentence: _____

7. Atlantic   New Word: _____   Meaning: _____
   Sentence: _____

8. arrange   New Word: _____   Meaning: _____
   Sentence: _____

9. marine   New Word: _____   Meaning: _____
   Sentence: _____

10. shine   New Word: _____   Meaning: _____
    Sentence: _____

Name: _____   **Date:** _____

A suffix is a letter or group of letters added to the end of a word to make a new word. Many suffixes change the part of speech of the word to which they are added.

SUFFIXES THAT FORM NOUNS		
Base Word	**Suffix**	**Noun**
cooperate (verb)	–ion	cooperation
specialize (verb)	–ation	specialization
wise (adjective)	–dom	wisdom
relation (noun)	–ship	relationship

SUFFIXES THAT FORM ADJECTIVES		
Base Word	**Suffix**	**Adjective**
solve (verb)	–able, –ible	solvable
suffice (verb)	–ant, –ent, –ient	sufficient
silk (noun)	–en	silken
cooperate (verb)	–ive, _ative, _itive	cooperative

Notice that sometimes a letter or letters must be dropped from the base word when adding a suffix. For example, the final *e* of *wise* is dropped when forming the noun *wisdom.*

Directions: Add a suffix to each word. Use a dictionary to make sure the new word is a real word. Then write the meaning of the new word and use it in a sentence.

1. wood   New Word: _____ Meaning: _____
   Sentence: _____

2. fest   New Word: _____ Meaning: _____
   Sentence: _____

3. realize   New Word: _____ Meaning: _____
   Sentence: _____

4. collect   New Word: _____ Meaning: _____
   Sentence: _____

5. free   New Word: _____ Meaning: _____
   Sentence: _____

6. friend   New Word: _____ Meaning: _____
   Sentence: _____

7. Mars   New Word: _____ Meaning: _____
   Sentence: _____

8. import   New Word: _____ Meaning: _____
   Sentence: _____

9. converse   New Word: _____ Meaning: _____
   Sentence: _____

10. admire   New Word: _____ Meaning: _____
    Sentence: _____

Name: _____   **Date:** _____

Homophones are words that have the same or nearly the same pronunciation. Homophones sound the same, but they differ in meaning and spelling.

main: chief; principal   **mane**: long growing on the neck of a horse or lion

The word "homograph" comes from two Greek words: "homo" (same) and "graphos" (to write). Homographs are words that have the same spelling but different meanings. Pairs of homographs might have different pronunciations, too.

bow: a tied ribbon   **bow**: to bend at the waist as a sign of respect
left: opposite of right   **left**: past tense of "leave"

Directions: The following sentences contain one or more misused homophones. Cross out each incorrect homophone and write the correct homophone above.

1. Wee were glad to here that you would lone us ten dollars.

2. "And over their," the guide explained, "is the thrown the king sat in during his rain."

3. "Oh, deer," Amy said as she sat at the piano. "I'm knot sure I no how to play that won."

4. The brown bare eight all the read berries.

5. The friends waived at each other when they past in the haul.

Directions: See if you can think a homograph for each pair of sentences below.

6. The _____ stepped up to the plate and waited for the pitcher to throw the baseball.

   Daphne licked the cake _____ off the spoon she used to mix it.

7. The _____ robbers jumped in the getaway car and sped off.

   The swans made their nest in the tall grass growing on the _____.

8. The old man on the stage coach was _____ for California.

   The gazelle _____ away, leaping through the tall grass.

9. This _____ sells shipping supplies to other companies.

   A _____ handshake gives a good impression.

10. What does *homograph* _____?

    Don't be _____ to your little sister!

The following words are sometimes used incorrectly. They may have similar spellings, pronunciations, or meanings that make them easy to confuse.

WORD	MEANING	EXAMPLE
affect	verb: to influence; to cause change in	Your eating habits affect your health.
effect	noun: result; outcome	What effect does smoking have on the lungs?
farther	more–refers to physical distance	My house is farther away than yours.
further	more–refers to time, amount, or degree	Let's think about this further.
accept	to agree to receive or do something	Please accept my apology.
except	not including; if not for the fact that	Tammy likes all vegetables except peas.
than	used in comparisons	I'm older than you.
then	after that; at some time in the past; in that case	First it rained. Then it snowed. If you don't like it, then don't eat it.
fewer	not as many–refers to countable objects	I have fewer marbles than you.
less	not as much–refers to measurable amounts	I have less food than you.

Directions: Underline the correct word in each set of parentheses.

1. The building is (farther, further) away (than, then) Jeff thought it was.
2. There were (fewer, less) people at the meeting (than, then) expected
3. How will the weather (affect, effect) our travel plans?
4. Gregory expected more problems with his science project, but there were actually (fewer, less).
5. After thinking about the problem (farther, further), the boss decided to fire everyone (accept, except) his top manager.
6. The improved engine produces (fewer, less) pollution.
7. The doctors tested my heart to see how the new medicine might (affect, effect) me.
8. I hope the teacher will (accept, except) my report even though it is late.
9. This interesting topic requires (farther, further) research.
10. The actors will (accept, except) their awards at the podium and (than, then) exit the stage.
11. I like everything about summer (accept, except) the mosquitoes.
12. We will walk to the store, rather (than, then) drive.
13. How much (farther, further) is it to the museum?
14. There is (fewer, less) money in my bank than I expected.
15. Warm weather can have a good (affect, effect) on people's spirits.

Name: _____ **Date:** _____

Words often create feelings and reactions. The feelings they suggest are called connotations. For example, both *car* and *limo* refer to four-wheeled automobiles. However, many people associate an image of luxury with the word *limo*. The word *car*, on the other hand, has neutral connotations. In other words, it does not create any special feelings. Compare these two sentences. Which creates a stronger feeling and image?

> The car rolled slowly past the crowd on the sidewalk.
> The limo rolled slowly past the crowd on the sidewalk.

Some words have negative connotations. Compare these two sentences.

> The thrifty shopper picked up a bag of potatoes.
> The penny-pinching shopper picked up a bag of potatoes.

Though the words "thrifty" and "penny-pinching" have the same basic meaning, a "thrifty" person is thought of as smart, but a "penny-pinching" person is thought of as stingy.

Directions: Complete each sentence by underlining one of the words in parentheses. Does the word you chose have a positive, neutral, or negative connotation? Write *Positive, Neutral,* or *Negative* on the line.

1. The fish's skin felt (slimy, slippery). _____

2. Mrs. Dunstable (cares, frets) about her son's grades at school. _____

3. Gina made a (jeering, teasing) remark about Malcolm's crush on his teacher.

   _____

4. The babysitter took the child (gruffly, firmly) by the hand. _____

5. What (reason, excuse) did the politician give for breaking his promise?

   _____

6. Sam's reaction to the unfortunate news was (cold, calm). _____

7. The candidate (challenged, attacked) the senator's viewpoint. _____

8. Tabitha did a (energetic, frenzied) dance. _____

9. Iris's performance in the play was (so-so, adequate). _____

10. Hannah (lied, misspoke) when she said she'd never broken a rule. _____

Directions: For each word, write a word with a similar meaning but a negative connotation.

11. Positive: antique   Negative: _____

12. Positive: fragrance   Negative: _____

13. Positive: self-confident   Negative: _____

14. Positive: ordinary   Negative: _____

15. Positive: borrow   Negative: _____

Name: _____   **Date:** _____

An idiom is a phrase with a special meaning. It does not mean exactly what the individual words in the phrase say. Often the meaning of an idiom can only be understood in context.

> Lisa bit off more than she could chew when she chose "the history of the world" as the topic of her research report.

The idiom *bite off more than you can chew* does not literally mean what it says. It means "attempt to do something that is beyond your ability."

Directions: The following items contain underlined idioms. Match the idioms with the meanings in the box. Write the letter of the correct meaning on the line.

A. reached its lowest point	F. earn money
B. easy to do	G. extremely crowded
C. go from one bad situation to another	H. dressed or decorated in a fancy way
D. reenergized	I. told a secret
E. began	J. perform well enough

1. ____ We thought building this model would be hard, but it turned out to be <u>a piece of cake</u>.

2. ____ After a delay of several months, construction on the new city hall <u>got off the ground</u> last April.

3. ____ Mr. Harlan's pep talk <u>gave a shot in the arm</u> to the tired volunteers, and they finished the cleanup in no time.

4. ____ The price of gasoline <u>bottomed out</u> in May but began to rise again in June.

5. ____ My mother works hard to <u>bring home the bacon</u> for her family.

6. ____ The prom-goers were <u>decked out</u> in tuxedos and satin gowns.

7. ____ The gym was <u>bursting at the seams</u> the night the district championship game was played.

8. ____ The party was supposed to be a surprise for Ms. Yancy, but Joe <u>spilled the beans</u> when she asked him why everyone seemed so secretive.

9. ____ Seana didn't make the team because she did not <u>cut the mustard</u>.

10. ____ Justin hated his job, but he <u>jumped out of the frying pan and into the fire</u> when he quit and then could not find another job.

Name: _____   **Date:** _____

Writers sometimes use similes and metaphors to help create a vivid image in the reader's mind. A **simile** compares two things using the word *like* or *as*.

Life is like a ride on a roller coaster.
My baby cousin is as sweet as candy.

A **metaphor** also compares two things, but it does not use the word *like* or *as*.

Life is a roller coaster ride.
This house is a prison.

Directions: Write *simile* or *metaphor* to tell what kind of language the writer has used in the sentences below.

1. Your unkind words are like razors. _____

2. Learning a new language can be a long, hard uphill climb. _____

3. The pavement was as hot as a frying pan. _____

4. After being away from home all those lonely weeks, even the sound of my brothers arguing was music to my ears. _____

5. The kitchen is the heart of Aunt Myra's house. _____

Directions: Complete each sentence with a simile. Use your imagination.

6. When the phone rang, Celie jumped _____.

7. As the curtain rose, Christian's heart pounded _____.

8. During the sad parts of the movie, Alexandra cried _____.

9. The idea struck Parnell _____.

10. "That music sounds like _____ Mr. Porter told his daughter.

11. The rumor traveled _____.

12. When Marcus puts styling gel in his hair, it feels _____.

13. As the storm approached, Mindy trembled _____.

14. The house sat on the hill _____.

15. The pain in Victor's foot _____.

BONUS: Think about each subject below and form an image of it in your mind. Then write a sentence containing a metaphor describing some aspect of it.

car _____

a mountain lion _____

an athlete _____

Name: _____   **Date:** _____

Synonyms are words with the same or nearly the same meanings. A *thesaurus* is a book that lists synonyms for entry words. Below is a sample thesaurus entry.

> **walk,** *v.,* **1.** step **2.** stroll **3.** stride **4.** trudge **5.** shuffle **6.** march **5.** waddle

While all the synonyms listed have the same basic meaning, each one has a different "shade" of meaning. Look at the different meanings the synonyms for *walk* give to this sentence: *She walked into the room.*

She **strolled** into the room.	She **strode** into the room.
She **trudged** into the room.	She **marched** into the room.
She **shuffled** into the room.	She **waddled** into the room.

If you were writing about a tired person, which sentence might you use? If you were writing about a calm, relaxed person, which would you use? You must read a thesaurus entry carefully before choosing a synonym that suits your idea.

Directions: Below is a list of thesaurus entries. Decide which synonym best matches the underlined word in each sentence and write it on the line. Use a different synonym in each sentence.

> **look,** *v.,* **1.** regard **2.** examine **3.** glance **4.** stare **5.** peek **6.** gaze **7.** glare **8.** observe
> **bad,** *adj.,* **1.** defective **2.** wicked **3.** lousy **4.** incorrect **5.** harmful **6.** unwell
>   **7.** spoiled **8.** unfortunate

1. Corlisa spent the rainy afternoon <u>looking</u> out the window. _____

2. The scientist <u>looked</u> at his invention, trying to find any flaws or defects. _____

3. Parents must teach their children that it is not polite to <u>look</u> at people. _____

4. Perry <u>looked</u> out from behind the curtain, hoping that Tanisa wouldn't see him in his hiding place. _____

5. The movie was so <u>bad</u> that Michael walked out in the middle of it. _____

6. This yogurt is <u>bad</u>. See the mold growing on it? _____

7. This new TV remote is <u>bad</u>, so I'm going to return it to the store. _____

8. The newspaper <u>said</u> that the fire damaged six buildings in all. _____

9. Ronald <u>says</u> that he can do a backflip off the diving board, but I don't believe him. _____

10. "Gosh, what beautiful weather we're having," Mr. Maxwell <u>said</u>. _____

Name: _____   **Date:** _____

The word "encyclopedia" comes from two Greek words meaning "general education." An encyclopedia provides information about every topic from aardvarks to zoot suits. Encyclopedia books, or volumes, are labeled alphabetically. Sometimes there is a separate volume for each letter of the alphabet, 26 books in all. At other times, there is too much information to fit in one volume, so the publishers "split" the letter between two volumes. For example, the first volume might be labeled "Aa–An" and the second volume, "Ao–Az."

Research Guide

Looking up a topic in an encyclopedia is a good first step in any research project. The best place to start your research is with the research guide that comes with most encyclopedias. A research guide is like an index. The topics in a research guide are listed alphabetically. Begin by looking up your topic, making sure you have the correct spelling. Here is an example of a research guide entry for "spaghetti" from *World Book Encyclopedias.*

> **Spaghetti**
> Pasta **P:192**

The above entry tells readers to look on page 192 of the volume labeled "P." If maps, pictures, or other supplementary information are included with the topic, the research guide lists them right after the volume and page number.

> **Spain So:730** *with pictures and maps*

The above entry tells readers to look on page 730 of the "So" volume. Some topics are large enough to include several subtopics. Here is a partial entry for *space travel* from the *World Book* Research Guide.

> **Space travel So: 694** *with pictures and maps*
> See also the Reading and Study Guide on this topic
> Altitude **A:394**
> Astronomy (Space Education) **A:848–849**
> Computer (In Engineering) **CI:912** *with picture*
> Cosmic Rays (Effects of Cosmic Rays) **CI:1077**

Notice the reference to the Reading and Study Guide on space travel. Popular research topics, such as space travel, are often accompanied by such guides. A Reading and Study Guide, shown on the same page as the topic, provides related topics for study. Here are some possible related topics for this subject.

> *How do astronauts and cosmonauts eat, sleep, and exercise on extended space missions? What problems have been posed by weightlessness? What other health problems do human beings face in space travel?*

Directions: Choose a topic that interests you and look it up in the research guide of a set of encyclopedias. Then, on a separate sheet of paper, list five possible related topics for the topic.

Name: _____   **Date:** _____

Dictionaries give definitions of words. The words are listed in alphabetical order. The two words at the top of a dictionary page are called guide words. They are the first and last words defined on the page. Any word that comes alphabetically between the guide words will be found on that page.

The words that are defined in a dictionary are called entry words. They are usually printed in dark type with dots separating the syllables of the word.

The entry word is followed by a pronunciation guide and the part of speech. The definitions come next. If an entry word has more than one definition, each definition will start with a number. If a word can be more than one part of speech, the dictionary will usually give a definition for each part of speech.

The etymology, or history, of a word may be shown in brackets at the end of an entry.

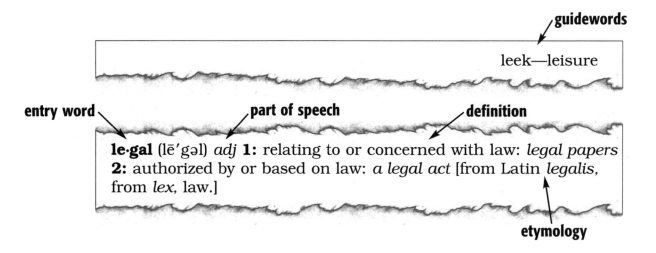

guidewords

leek—leisure

entry word   **part of speech**   **definition**

le·gal (lē′gəl) *adj* **1:** relating to or concerned with law: *legal papers* **2:** authorized by or based on law: *a legal act* [from Latin *legalis,* from *lex,* law.]

etymology

Choosing the correct definition

Where more than one meaning is listed, how do you decide which meaning applies to your word? Following these steps might help.

1. Decide how the word is used in the sentence. Is it a noun, a verb, or another part of speech?

2. If it is a noun, read all the definitions listed after the noun form of the word. If not, read the other appropriate definitions.

3. Now imagine that the word in the sentence is replaced with a blank line.

4. Substitute each definition into the sentence. The definition you are looking for is most likely the one that makes the most sense.

Directions: Answer the questions about the following dictionary guidewords and entries.

nephrite—neural

ner·o·li (nĕ′ə lē) *n* An essential oil distilled from orange flowers and used in making perfume [French; it was introduced into France around 1680 by Anna Maria de la Tremoille, princess of Neroli.]

nerve (nûrv) *n* **1:** any of the bundles of fibers connecting the central nervous system and the parts of the body **2:** strong will, courage: *It took nerve to stand up to that bully.* [Latin *nervus*, sinew, nerve.]

nest (nĕst) *n* **1: a.** a structure made by a bird for holding its eggs and its young **b.** the structure or place where fish or insects lay their eggs or keep their young **2:** a set of objects, such as decorative boxes, of graduated size, that can be stacked one inside the other *v* **1:** to build or occupy a nest [Middle English *nest*, Old English *nest*.]

nes·tle (nĕs′əl) *v* **1.** to settle snugly and comfortably: *The children nestled in their bed.* [Middle English *nestlen*, Old English *nestlian*, to make a nest.]

net·tle (nĕt′l) *n* **1:** any plant of the genus Urtica, having spiny leaves that sting the skin on contact *v* **1:** to irritate, annoy [Middle English *nettle*, Old English *netle*.]

1. Which word comes from the name of a place? _____

2. What is the meaning of the Latin word lex? _____

3. What part of speech is "nestle"? _____

4. From what language did the word "nerve" originate? _____

5. Look at the guidewords. Would the entry for the word *Neptune* fall before this page, on this page, or after this page? _____

6. How many definitions for the noun "nest" are given? _____

7. How many parts of speech are given for the word "nettle"? _____

8. When did the word *neroli* enter the French language? _____

Name: _____   Date: _____

All sentences are made up of clauses. A clause is a group of words that has a subject and a predicate. Both the subject and the predicate can be either simple or compound. A clause that can stand on its own as a sentence and expresses a complete thought is called an independent clause.

Sam showed up late. His shoes and jeans were muddy.

A dependent clause has a subject and predicate, but it cannot stand on its own as a sentence.

because it's raining   although he was tired   if you make the team

A dependent clause is always part of a longer sentence. It explains or gives more information about the thought expressed in the independent clause.

Independent   **Dependent**   **Dependent**   Independent

The curtain rose **after the lights dimmed**.   **When it was over,** we all applauded.

Most dependent clauses begin with a subordinating conjunction.

COMMON SUBORDINATING CONJUNCTIONS

after, although, as, as soon as, as though, because, before, even though, if, since, so that, unless, until, when, whenever, where, wherever, while

Directions: Label the underlined clause in each sentence *Independent* or *Dependent*.

1. Mom nearly fainted <u>when we jumped up and yelled "Surprise!"</u> _____
2. <u>After the sun went down</u>, the air became very humid. _____
3. <u>Jim peeled the potatoes</u> while he waited for the water to boil. _____
4. The basement floods <u>whenever it rains a lot</u>. _____
5. As soon as the turkey comes out of the over, <u>we will eat</u>. _____

Directions: Underline the dependent clause in each sentence. Circle the coordinating conjunction.

6. Some people spread happiness wherever they go.
7. Alyssa agreed to babysit tonight even though she has a lot of homework to do.
8. You look as though you could use a nap.
9. If we don't get to the airport in ten minutes, we'll miss our flight.
10. The kids went out to play flashlight tag as soon as it got dark.
11. We'll just stay home tonight, unless you can think of something fun to do.
12. Enrique's parents let him play video games whenever he wants.
13. As soon as the lettuce sprouted, rabbits came and ate it all.
14. Put a rock on the edge of the tablecloth so that it doesn't blow away.
15. If I see Simon at the mall, I'll give him your message.

Name: _____ **Date:** _____

There are four kinds of sentences in the English language: simple, compound, complex, and compound-complex. All are made up of clauses. A **simple** sentence consists of one independent clause. Remember, in any clause both the subject and the predicate can be either simple or compound.

KIND OF SENTENCE	EXAMPLE
Simple: consists of one independent clause	Patrice and her teammates swam for an hour.
Compound: two or more independent clauses joined by a coordinating conjunction *(and, or, but)*	Crickets sang in the grass, **and** an owl could be heard in the distance.
Complex: one independent clause and one or more dependent clauses	Lashon missed the bus **because he overslept**.
Compound-Complex: two or more independent clauses and at least one dependent clause	**After the game ended**, the crowd went home **and** crews began cleaning the stadium.

Directions: Label each sentence *Simple, Compound, Complex,* or *Compound-Complex.*

1. _____ Patrice swam the length of the pool and then practiced diving.

2. _____ Celine had a bad cold, so she stayed home from school today.

3. _____ There's no bread and the cereal is all gone, so you'll have to have something else for breakfast.

4. _____ Our teacher gave us a huge assignment, but it was actually pretty easy.

5. _____ Native speakers of English sometimes use incorrect grammar.

6. _____ The old man sat on the park bench and fed the squirrels.

7. _____ Although he has never had formal lessons, Julio plays the piano quite well, and his violin skills aren't bad either.

8. _____ Rashad volunteers at the nursing home whenever he has some spare time.

9. _____ Even though he put it safely in his pocket, Ted lost his lunch ticket.

10. _____ That printer doesn't work, but you can use the one in the office.

11. _____ The puppy chewed on my shoe and whined all night, but he's awfully cute anyway.

12. _____ Spiders and other creepy creatures have always scared and fascinated people.

13. _____ Because we had no candles, we sat in the dark when the electricity went out.

14. _____ If Bryson does not win the election, Vickie will be very disappointed.

Name: _____ **Date:** _____

All sentences are made up of independent and/or dependent clauses.

KIND OF SENTENCE	EXAMPLE
Simple: consists of one independent clause	Guatemala is a beautiful country.
Compound: two or more independent clauses joined by a coordinating conjunction (*and, or, but*)	Mayans built great palaces 2000 years ago, and they can still be seen today.
Complex: one independent clause and one or more dependent clauses	Because the land is very fertile, Guatemala depends a lot on agriculture.
Compound-Complex: two or more independent clauses and at least one dependent clause	The ruins of Tikal include over 3000 structures, but the most famous are the pyramids, and tourists come from all over the world to see them.

Directions: Read the paragraphs. Each sentence has a number. Decide if each sentence is simple, compound, complex, or compound-complex. Write the number of each sentence in the appropriate box below.

Guatemala

1. Guatemala is in Central America and borders Mexico, El Salvador, Honduras, and Belize. 2. The Caribbean Sea lies to the east of Guatemala, and the Pacific Ocean lies to the west. 3. A huge tropical forest covers most of the northern part of the country, and densely populated highlands occupy the southern region. 4. Coffee accounts for a large part of the country's revenue, and sugar and bananas are also valued exports, but industry is also important.

5. Guatemala is a land of contrasts. 6. Although Guatemala City, the country's capital, has all the makings of a modern city, some villages were settled by the Spaniards as early as the 1500s. 7. The biggest tourist attraction in Guatemala is in Tikal, where you can see ancient pyramids. 8. They were built by the Mayans. 9. While the Mayans are perhaps best known today for their great temples and ornate palaces, they were brilliant artists and mathematicians, and they excelled in astronomy as well. 10. The civilization mysteriously collapsed around 900 A.D., but Mayan descendents still populate Guatemala today.

SIMPLE	COMPOUND
COMPLEX	**COMPOUND-COMPLEX**

Name: _____   **Date:** _____

After you write a paragraph or a paper, it is important to revise your work. As you know, a complete sentence has a subject and a predicate and expresses a complete thought. A sentence that does not express a complete thought is called a sentence fragment. A sentence fragment may either be missing a subject or a verb, or it might be a prepositional phrase or a dependent clause.

Sentence Fragments
Will present the prize to the person who sells the most popcorn. (missing a subject)
Between the mountains and the sea. (prepositional phrase)
After Lu took the math final. (dependent clause)
Zoe appreciates. (missing a direct object)

Directions: Write *S* after every group of words that is a complete sentence.
Write *F* after every group of words that is a sentence fragment.

1. When Terrell got home, he began studying for his English exam. ____

2. Even though it embarrassed him. ____

3. Gerry went home and took a nap right after he finished his paper. ____

4. The principal will present the prize to the winner of the essay contest. ____

5. Stayed away from the abandoned building. ____

6. The horse that won the Kentucky Derby this year was stolen. ____

7. Jayla believes that her method is right. ____

8. Looked as if he had seen a ghost. ____

9. When he found out the truth about the missing money. ____

10. Because she hadn't heard of them before now. ____

Directions: Add words to these sentence fragments to make them complete sentences.

11. Through the back alleys of the city.

_____

12. Ever since I was a little kid.

_____

13. Before you leave for the day.

_____

14. But I've never been there before.

_____

15. If you want to.

_____

Name: _____   **Date:** _____

Do not join two sentences with only a comma.

A run-on sentence occurs when two or more sentences are combined as one. Run-on sentences are missing the proper punctuation needed to separate the ideas. One way to correct a run-on sentence is to write each complete thought as a separate sentence.

Run-on: Len said he hit his bunny phone he meant to say "funny bone."

Correct: Len said he hit his bunny phone. He meant to say "funny bone."

Another way to fix it is to join the two complete thoughts in a way that is correct. You can use conjunctions such as *and, but, or, because, so,* and *when* to join sentences.

Correct: When Len said he hit his bunny phone, he meant to say "funny bone."

Directions: Use proofreading marks to show how these run-on sentences can be corrected.

1. A spoonerism is the switching of sounds in two words, one example is saying "bunch lox" instead of "lunch box."

2. William Archibald Spooner was born in London in 1844 he was a dean and president at Oxford University.

3. Spooner was a kind, well-liked man, he was somewhat absent-minded.

4. His brain was so keen that his tongue often could not keep up with it he frequently switched the beginning sounds of words.

5. For example, he scolded one student for "hissing my mystery lecture" he then added, "You have tasted the whole worm."

6. He made other mistakes, he once spoke of the "kinquering congs."

7. Sometimes he mixed up sounds at church he once told the groom during a wedding, "Son, it is now kisstomary to cuss the bride."

8. He once found a woman sitting in his place at church he said, "Pardon me, madam, I believe you're occupewing my pie."

9. He asked her "Shall I sew you to another sheet?" she was probably laughing too hard to move.

10. Spooner died in 1930 at the age of 86 his legacy lives on in the term "Spoonerism."

Name: _____   **Date:** _____

Directions: This paragraph contains sentence fragments and run-on sentences. Underline them, and then write them correctly on the lines below.

The Legend of Paris

Long ago, the king and queen of Troy received a message from the gods. The queen was having a baby boy soon, the gods warned that the boy would one day cause the destruction of Troy. So when Paris was born. The king commanded that he be left on a hillside to die. However, the baby didn't die. He was found by a shepherd and his wife they raised him as their son.

A few years later, there was an important wedding party all the gods and goddesses, except the goddess Discord, were invited. Discord was angry. Because she hadn't been invited. She thought of a way to disrupt the wedding party. She made an apple with the words "To the Fairest Goddess" on it, she tossed it into the crowd at the party.

Each of the goddesses at the party was sure the apple was intended for her. Hera, queen of the gods, argued. With her beautiful daughters Athena and Aphrodite. Which one deserved the apple? They argued bitterly, they could not agree. Finally they asked King Zeus to decide. He refused to take sides. Instead, he sent a messenger to find a shepherd to make the decision. The messenger returned with a shepherd it was Paris. Nobody knew who he really was, though.

Each goddess offered Paris a gift. If he would choose her. Hera offered him a powerful kingdom, Athena offered him military power. Aphrodite, the goddess of love, offered him the most beautiful woman in the world, Queen Helen of Greece. Paris could not resist that offer, he gave the apple to Aphrodite. With the protection of Aphrodite. Paris kidnapped Helen and took her to Troy. Once there, he learned of his noble birth.

Because Paris had stolen their queen. The leaders of Greece were angry. They led their armies to Troy to rescue Helen. Thus one of the most famous wars in all of history, the Trojan War, began. And the gods' prediction came true.

When you revise, look out for short, choppy sentences. Too many can make your writing seem dull. They can be improved in several ways. One way is to join short sentences to make longer compound sentences. If the ideas in the sentences are related, combine them with a comma and a coordinating conjunction *(and, but, or)* to form a compound sentence. You might also combine them with a subordinating conjunction *(after, although, as, as soon as, as though, because, before, even though, if, since, so that, unless, until, when, whenever, where, wherever, while)* to create a complex or compound-complex sentence. Combining sentences can help make your writing smoother and easier to read.

CHOPPY: Steve graduated from college. Then he started his own business.
COMPOUND: Steve graduated from college, and then he started his own business.
COMPLEX: After Steve graduated from college, he started his own business.

Directions: Combine each pair of sentences to create a compound or complex sentence.

1. Nina tried on the dress. She decided it looked better on the hanger.

   _____

2. Kanesha has a hard time studying at home. Her siblings are noisy.

   _____

3. Eric goes for a run every morning. Then he has breakfast.

   _____

4. That director has made several movies. They were all popular.

   _____

5. Every weekend, Mrs. Chen washes the clothes. Her husband folds them.

   _____

6. The sign was faded. We could still make out the words "Sam's Soda Shoppe."

   _____

7. Clay had trouble playing the song. He hadn't practiced it much.

   _____

8. Roger managed to find a seat in the waiting room. It was crowded.

   _____

9. This building used to be the county jail. Later, it was turned into a library.

   _____

10. The truck overturned on the sharp curve. Hundreds of chickens escaped.

    _____

Name: _____   **Date:** _____

Too many short, choppy sentences can make your writing hard to read. To avoid this, combine short sentences that have the same subject.
CHOPPY: Scott spent an hour studying the chapter. He did well on the test.
SMOOTH: Scott spent an hour studying the chapter and did well on the test.
SMOOTH: Because he spent an hour studying the chapter, Scott did well on the test.

You can also combine sentences that have the same predicate.
CHOPPY: Tron volunteered to take tickets. He volunteered to work concessions. He volunteered to serve as an usher.
SMOOTH: Tron volunteered to take tickets, work concessions, and serve as an usher.

Directions: Combine the following groups of sentences. You may add or delete words as needed but do not change the meaning.

1. Gina had a toothache. She went to the dentist.

   _____

2. The movie was about mountain climbing. The movie took place in Nepal.

   _____

3. Paulina visited Germany and Hungary. She also visited Poland.

   _____

4. Euphemia sprained her ankle at practice. She won't be able to play Friday.

   _____

5. Sinbad yearned for the smell of the sea. He yearned for the call of gulls. Most of all, he yearned most for the sight of sails billowing in the wind.

   _____

6. Reggie wrote the company a letter of complaint. He never received a reply.

   _____

7. The old horse spent its days grazing in the meadow. It spent its days basking in the warm sun. It spent its nights sleeping in the snug stall in the barn.

   _____

8. Mr. Bartlett baked three pumpkin pies for the bake sale. He also baked a chocolate cake. He also baked a batch of oatmeal cookies.

   _____

9. Jana didn't like watermelon. She ate it anyway.

   _____

10. Olivia gave Pam a necklace. She also gave Pam a beach towel.

   _____

Name: _____   **Date:** _____

A few short sentences in your writing are fine, but too many can make your writing sound choppy and repetitive. Two or more short sentences with the same subject or predicate can often be combined into one sentence.

Directions: Combine the following groups of sentences. You may add or delete words as needed but do not change the basic meaning.

1. Shamus told a story. He used different voices for the characters. He entertained the children.

   _____

2. Lily kicked the ball. She ran as fast as she could. She made it to second base.

   _____

3. The heavy rains flooded the lowlands. They swelled the riverbanks. They caused a mudslide.

   _____

4. The council approved the plans. The mayor approved the plans. Finally, the voters approved the plans as well.

   _____

5. The guard dog lowered its head. The guard dog growled. The guard dog bared its teeth. The guard dog attacked the intruder.

   _____

6. People from Ireland arrived at Ellis Island. Italians and Hungarians arrived at Ellis Island.

   _____

7. Backgammon is a very old game. Backgammon requires both skill and luck.

   _____

8. Diedre contacted the animal shelter. She spoke to her neighbors. She searched everywhere for her dog.

   _____

9. Fish populations dwindled. Crab and shrimp populations dwindled as well.

   _____

10. Alima sang in front of 300 people. She was nervous. She sang flawlessly.

    _____

Name: _____   **Date:** _____

Sometimes you can combine two sentences by moving a descriptive word or phrase from one sentence to the other. You might need to make a small change to a word before moving it. In the sentences below, notice that the verb *sparkles* was changed to the adjective *sparkly*, the adjective *annoying* was changed to the adverb *annoyingly*, and the verb *ached* was changed to the adjective *aching*.

TWO SENTENCES	COMBINED
We saw a play last night. It was **terrific**.	We saw a **terrific** play last night.
Kyle got a letter. It was **from Jason**.	Kyle got a letter **from Jason**.
Mia wears nailpolish. It **sparkles**.	Mia wears **sparkly** nailpolish.
The door squeaks. It is **annoying**.	The door squeaks **annoyingly**.
Lisa put ice on her knee. It **ached**.	Lisa put ice on her **aching** knee.

Directions: Combine each set of sentences by moving the underlined part to the first sentence. You may need to change the form of the underlined part.

1. Tran dropped his lunch tray. It fell <u>on the floor</u>.

   _____

2. Jorge fixed the broken cup. He did it <u>with a special glue for ceramics</u>.

   _____

3. The police tried to calm the crowd. The crowd was <u>unruly</u>.

   _____

4. Chris turned his nose up at the French fries. They were <u>greasy</u>.

   _____

5. David tossed and turned on the mattress. It was full of <u>lumps</u>.

   _____

6. The seamstress made a dress from an old tablecloth. She was an <u>expert</u>.

   _____

7. The faucet dripped incessantly. It <u>leaked</u>.

   _____

8. Grandma took an old photo off the shelf. It was covered with <u>dust</u>.

   _____

9. Gary found the application form. It was <u>on top of the refrigerator</u>.

   _____

10. Have you seen the library on Colorado Street? It's <u>new</u>.

    _____

Name: _____   **Date:** _____

An appositive is a word or phrase that describes a noun. These two sentences both contain information about Eric. You can combine them by using the words *an avid animal lover* as an appositive. Be sure to set off the appositive with commas.

Eric had a great time at the zoo. He's an avid animal lover.
Eric, an avid animal lover, had a great time at the zoo.

Appositives may appear at the end or in the middle of a sentence. Be sure to place the appositive directly after the noun or noun phrase it describes.

Eric loved the caracal. A caracal is a wild cat of Africa and southern Asia.
Eric loved the caracal, a wild cat of Africa and southern Asia.

Directions: Combine each pair of sentences by using words in the second sentence to make an appositive. Remember to use commas to set off the appositive in the new sentence.

1. Iris made the appetizers and Jonah made the main course. The appetizers were stuffed cherry tomatoes.

   _____

2. Jack's father put up track lights in the bedroom. He is an expert electrician.

   _____

3. The hosts welcomed the guests. The hosts were the Jenkins.

   _____

4. Laura's mother served her favorite dish at the dinner to celebrate Laura's graduation. Her favorite dish is lasagna.

   _____

5. At the museum, we saw a copy of the Mona Lisa. The Mona Lisa is a famous painting by Leonardo da Vinci.

   _____

6. Alexis has a photo of The Bugs in her locker. The Bugs is her favorite band.

   _____

7. Hannah enjoys lying in the sun and watching birds. Hannah is Amy's dog.

   _____

8. Humphrey Bogart is often pictured wearing a trenchcoat and fedora. Humphrey Bogart was a famous tough-guy actor of the 30's and 40's.

   _____

9. The crown was set with sapphires and rubies. Sapphires are blue gemstones.

   _____

Name: _____   **Date:** _____

An introductory phrase is a group of words that begins a sentence. The phrase should be set off by a comma. Sometimes it is possible to combine two related sentences by turning one into an introductory phrase. Begin the phrase with the *–ing* or *–ed* form of the verb in the sentence.

    Two Sentences: The waiters sang while they worked.
    They entertained the customers.
    One Sentence With an Introductory Phrase: Singing while they worked, the waiters entertained the customers.
An introductory phrase must relate to the noun that follows it.
    WRONG: Singing while they worked, the customers were entertained by the waiters. (This sentence suggests that the customers were singing and working!)

Directions: Combine each pair of sentences by turning the underlined sentence into an introductory phrase.
    EXAMPLE: <u>The baby smiled with delight</u>. She listened to her mother sing.
    Smiling with delight, the baby listened to her mother sing.

1. The golfers headed to the clubhouse. <u>They were tired of the rain showers</u>.

   _____

2. The singer introduced her next song. <u>She strummed her guitar lightly</u>.

   _____

3. <u>We were strolling by the lake</u>. We saw lots of ducks.

   _____

4. The angry customer left. <u>He was disgusted with the poor service</u>.

   _____

5. The firefighters finally put the fire out. <u>They had worked around the clock</u>.

   _____

6. <u>The puppy was frightened by the fireworks</u>. He hid under the lawn chairs.

   _____

7. Henry carried his bowl to the living room. <u>He was spilling soup the whole way</u>.

   _____

8. The child ran to his mother. <u>He was crying but unhurt</u>.

   _____

9. The elderly senator simply waved to the audience and smiled. <u>He was embarrassed by the applause</u>.

   _____

10. <u>Eva ran as fast as she could</u>. She reached the grocery store in five minutes.

   _____

Name: _____   **Date:** _____

Short sentences can be made longer by adding details in the form of adjectives, adverbs, or prepositional phrases. Adding details can make your writing more interesting and more informative. Look at these examples.

The cat meowed.
The **orange, battle-scarred** cat meowed. (adjectives)
The orange, battle-scarred cat meowed **eerily**. (adverb)
The orange, battle-scarred cat meowed eerily **in the alley at midnight**. (prepositional phrases)

As you can see by the above examples, details can make sentences more interesting, and they allow the reader to better understand the writer's ideas.

Directions: Expand the sentences by adding one or more adjective, adverb, and prepositional phrase to each one.

1. The dinosaur trudged. _____

2. Latoya carried the gerbil. _____

3. The tractor rusted. _____

4. I forgot my baseball glove. _____

5. The thief tiptoed. _____

6. The car disappeared. _____

7. Mr. Appleby complained. _____

8. The honey bees gathered pollen. _____

9. Rafe gave the teacher his paper. _____

10. The whales beached themselves. _____

Name: _____ **Date:** _____

In the active voice, the subject of the sentence is the "doer" of the verb action. The action of the verb is directed towards the direct object. In the passive voice, the direct object is the subject, and the "doer" is the receiver of the verb.

Active Voice: Mrs. Kent took Lisa to the mall.

Passive Voice: Lisa was taken to the mall by Mrs. Kent.

In general, it is best to use the active voice more often than the passive voice. The active voice usually expresses the meaning of a sentence more clearly and strongly. However, you can use the passive when the performer of the action is unknown or unimportant.

Two banks were robbed yesterday.

(Better than *Somebody robbed two banks yesterday.*)

You can also use the passive when what happened to the object is the most important part of the sentence.

Residents have been advised to lock their doors and be on the lookout.

Directions: Read each pair of sentences. Both sentences in each pair express the same idea. Which one expresses the idea best? Underline that sentence.

1. Sandy is easily frightened./Things frighten Sandy easily.

2. The lights were left on by Lisa again./Lisa left the lights on again.

3. I lost your keys./Your keys were lost by me.

4. Hunters have hunted these beautiful creatures nearly to extinction./ These beautiful creatures have been hunted nearly to extinction.

5. Workers completed the tower in 1753./The tower was completed in 1753.

Directions: If the sentence is in the passive voice, rewrite it in the active. If the sentence is in the active voice, rewrite it in the passive.

6. The pink purse was given to Abby by me.

_____

7. Shoppers can find men's clothing on the third floor.

_____

8. All safety rules must be followed by employees.

_____

9. A bee stung Morgan.

_____

10. Another hurricane has hit the east coast.

_____

Name: _____   **Date:** _____

As you know, the tense of a verb tells whether the action happens in the past, present, or future. Sometimes writers make mistakes in verb tense when writing. That is why it is important to check the tenses of your verbs when you revise your writing. Using the wrong tense or shifting tense unexpectedly can make your message unclear.

Incorrect: When Drew looked up, he sees a strange light in the sky.
Correct: When Drew looked up, he saw a strange light in the sky.

Directions: The underlined sentences in this story might contain mistakes in verb tense. Circle each incorrect verb. On a separate sheet of paper, write it correctly.

"Hey, Collin!" Drew yelled. "Guess what happened after I left your house last night!"

"What?" Collin asked, walking up to Drew.

"Well, I was walking home, and I see this light in the sky," Drew began.

"Really? What kind of light was it?" Collin asked.

Drew shook his head and said, "I couldn't tell for sure. It just looks like a red glow. It seems to be coming from that empty lot on Longview Drive."

Collin frowned. "A red glow?" he repeated. "Well, what was it?"

Drew looked at Collin sheepishly. "I think maybe it was a UFO."

"A UFO? You're kidding!" Collin snorted.

Drew looked hurt. "Hey, don't laugh," he said. "It was weird."

"Okay, I'm sorry. So tell me— why did you think it was a UFO?" Collin asked.

Drew stopped and held Collin by the arm. "Because I walk across the lot to find the source of the light—and there wasn't anything!" he said, his face serious. "The sky is just glowing right above the lot, and there was no reason for it."

"Maybe it was one of those beacons from that car dealership downtown," Collin suggested.

"I don't think so," Drew replied.

Collin was thoughtful for a moment. "Do you see anything besides a glow?" he asked.

"Hmm… I notice a flash of blue light out of the corner of my eye," Drew said. "And then the light was gone, just like that." He snapped his fingers.

The boys walked in silence for a few moments, and then Collin spoke. "I'll tell you what—let's go check it out together tonight?" Collin suggested.

Drew smiled with relief. "That would be great. You should bring your camera, just in case."

Name: _____ Date: _____

There are two major steps to writing a paper: deciding on a topic and then figuring out what to write about the topic. The first step is usually pretty easy, especially if your teacher assigns the topic. But the second step can be more difficult. Here are a few methods to use to generate ideas about a topic.

Free writing   Free writing involves writing nonstop on your topic for a few minutes. Put the name of your topic at the top of the page and then start writing any words, phrases, or sentences that come to mind. When finished, glance over what you've written and select what you think is the most important word, phrase, or idea. Free write about that word, phrase, or idea for a few more minutes. Repeat as necessary. Afterwards, you should have some useful ideas.

Talking with others   "Bounce" your ideas off friends, teachers, and family members. Be open to their perspectives. Take notes, and then free write on any ideas that interest you.

Reading   Reading stimulates thinking, so find out what others have written about the topic. Scan books, encyclopedia entries, magazine articles, and Internet sources. List important or interesting points they make. One may lead toward a topic.

Listing   Make a list of everything that comes to mind about your topic. Simply jot down every word or short phrase that occurs to you. Once you've exhausted your ideas, arrange the items in the list in categories. Then assign a category name. You may add to the list as you're working or eliminate any items that don't fit in. One of your categories may be an ideal topic for your paper.

Studying an encyclopedia   Check the research guide that comes with a set of encyclopedias. The research guide often provides a list of subtopics for a main topic. The list of subtopics could provide you with a suitable direction for your paper.

Directions: On a separate sheet of paper, use one of the above methods to generate ideas about one of the following topics. When you're finished, share the possible topics you generated with the class.

Choose one:

Why Be a Volunteer?   Zoos   Why Sports Are Important

Name: _____   Date: _____

A graphic organizer is a "picture of information." Using a graphic organizer in the early stages of writing a paper can help you generate and organize your ideas. Below are two of the most common organizers for writing.

An idea web is helpful for quickly coming up with ideas about a topic.

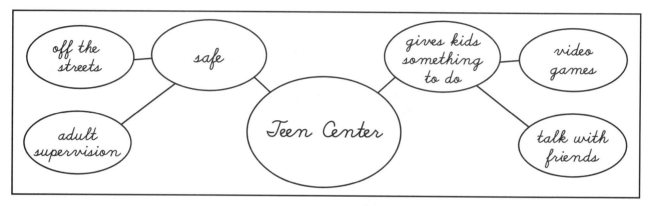

A Venn diagram is useful for comparing and contrasting.

Value of Sports
teaches good
sportsmanship;
teaches cooperation;
provides fun;
provides physical
activity

give students
life skills;
provide social
interaction;
teach
responsibility

Value of School
prepares students
for life; helps
students become
problem-solvers;
prepares students
for careers

Directions: Choose one of the following topics. On a separate sheet of paper, use one of the graphic organizers above to explore it.

- Extending the school day by an hour
- Allowing/not allowing children to play with toy weapons
- Compare/contrast two leisure-time activities of your choice
- Compare/contrast middle school to elementary school

Name: _____   **Date:** _____

A paragraph is a group of sentences that relate to one topic. Most paragraphs contain a topic sentence that states the topic of the paragraph. Topic sentences normally fall at the beginning of the paragraph.

The topic sentence is followed by sentences that support it. These supporting sentences contain details—examples, facts, opinions, comparisons, descriptions, etc.—that relate to and support the topic sentence.

Paragraphs usually end with a concluding statement. This "conclusion" rephrases the topic sentence, or expresses it in a different way while making the same point. Often the conclusion is a strong statement meant to make readers remember the writer's ideas.

The topic sentence and the conclusion in the following paragraph are underlined. The sentences in between are supporting details.

Immigrants are beneficial to the United States. For example, immigrants start many of the small businesses in the country each year. These small businesses create jobs for all Americans. In addition, immigrants buy American goods and services, which helps boost the economy. They also pay billions in taxes every year. Finally, immigrants contribute to all aspects of society, from agriculture to art to education to food to music to technology. In so many ways, the people who come to the United States from other lands help make this country a good place to live.

Directions: The sentences of the following paragraph are out of order. First, identify the topic sentence. Then number the sentences 1–7 to show the correct order, starting with the topic sentence.

_____ Once they arrive in the new country, they must adapt to a culture whose language and customs they may not know.

_____ Immigrants to a new country have many difficult adjustments to make in their daily lives.

_____ Simple things such as ordering in a restaurant, shopping, or even getting a haircut can suddenly become frustrating tasks.

_____ In short, immigrants face many changes and challenges when adjusting to their new home country.

_____ For example, immigrants must leave behind everyone they know—friends, relatives, classmates, neighbors, etc.—knowing they may never see these people again.

_____ In addition, many immigrants experience long periods of loneliness before they make new friends and feel as if they "fit in."

_____ What they eat, where they work, where they go to school or church, and where they shop may all change radically from the moment they leave their homelands.

Every piece of writing must have a main idea, or topic. Every detail within that piece of writing should directly support that topic. Any detail that does not support the topic should be omitted.

Sticking to Your Topic

- Write a clear topic sentence. Make sure your topic sentence reflects exactly what you want to write about.
- Keep the topic sentence in mind as you write. Refer back to it often, if necessary.
- Reread every detail sentence in your rough draft. If you find yourself struggling to see a relationship between a detail and the topic sentence, take out the detail.

Directions: The paragraphs below contain information unrelated to the topic sentence. Underline the topic sentence in each paragraph. Cross out the unrelated information.

The Cowboy's Life

Life as a cowboy in the Old West was not as glamorous as movies make it out to be. Many cowboys owned only their saddles and the clothes on their backs; many did not even own a horse! Some had an extra set of clothes and a spare pair of boots. Most made between $25 and $50 a month and were expected to work long hard hours for their meager pay. On cattle drives, for example, cowboys were expected to ride in wind, rain, heat, and blizzards to tend the herd. If need be they stayed up all night chasing down strays and then spent next day pulling cattle out of the mud with teams of oxen. Sometimes, though, the weather was nice and the cattle drive went well.

Life back at the ranch was equally hard. If they were lucky enough to be kept on between drives, the cowboys had an endless list of chores to do. From sunup to sundown, they branded livestock, broke horses, mended fences, and planted and harvested crops. Modern cowboys might have sophisticated machines and tools to  help with these sorts of chores. At the end of the day, the cowboys retired to their bunkhouses, often just sod shacks. During the summer they lived with lice and fleas in their bedding, and in the winter, they scraped ice off the walls and huddled around a wood stove for heat. A wood stove is not the most efficient way to heat a room. Hollywood portrays cowboys as free spirits roaming the range at their leisure, but in reality they were overworked, underpaid, and miserable much of the time.

Name: _____   Date: _____

Transitional words and phrases help readers see the connection between ideas.

Turn the heat on high to pop the popcorn. **While** the corn is popping, shake the pan occasionally to prevent burning. **After** all the kernels have popped, pour the popcorn into a bowl. **Then**, drizzle a tablespoon or two of butter over it.

Each transitional word or phrase has a special function. This chart shows just a few transitional words and phrases.

FUNCTION	EXAMPLES
To introduce a new idea	in addition, also, too, furthermore, another
To show cause and effect	because, so that, therefore, as a result, if . . . then
To introduce an example	for example, to illustrate, namely
To show the degree of importance	above all, most important, worse, worst, better, best
To introduce a summary	in conclusion, all in all, to summarize, on the whole
To show sequence in time	first, then, next year, the next day, in the future
To show comparison or contrast	however, although, on the other hand, likewise, in the same manner
To show spatial relations	there, here, at the top, underneath, behind

Directions: Read the travelogue and write an appropriate transition on each line.

We had a great time on our trip to Washington, D.C. On Monday, we took a 1-hour guided tour of the Pentagon. _____ we saw models of many military airplanes and ships and learned a little about the history of each branch of the service. Then we went to FBI headquarters. We took a tour there, _____. I was amazed by the spy equipment the FBI has used over the years. _____ we went out for dinner and then went back to our rooms for the night.

_____, we started the day by visiting Arlington National Cemetery, where veterans from the Revolutionary War to today are buried. _____ we went to the Ford Theater, where Abraham Lincoln was assassinated. That afternoon, we toured the monuments of Washington, Jefferson, and Lincoln. We _____ saw the Vietnam Wall and the Korean Memorial. After dinner, we visited the National Cathedral and heard an opera singer perform _____. We saw a lot that Tuesday!

A book report gives information and your opinion about a book you have read. When you write a book report, begin with an introduction that catches the reader's interest and tells the title of the book and the author's name. You might ask a question or give a quotation from the book to help interest the reader. The main part of the book report should tell a little of what the book is about. It might tell whether the book is sad, funny, or thrilling. It might also tell who the main characters are, or give a brief outline of the plot. You should also make it clear whether the book is fiction or nonfiction. Finally, tell your opinion of the book. Did you like it? Why? Would you recommend this book? Why or why not?

Directions: Shantay has written the following book report. Read it and answer the questions.

Ashley Simpson is the girl everyone envies. She seems to have it all—she's pretty, she gets good grades, she's a terrific gymnast, she's got lots of expensive clothes. As she snobbishly puts it, she's a "high quality" girl. Yet no one guesses that behind Ashley's cool smile lie deep troubles and secrets. Ashley is the main character of *The Smiles That Lie,* by Lianna Kersher. This book will slowly but surely draw you into the complicated world of Ashley.

One of the first things the reader learns about Ashley is that her mother is a powerful lawyer and her father is a wealthy stockbroker. Later it is revealed that they are divorced, and treat Ashley like a pawn in their fights. Ashley has an older brother that she talks about to her friends. She tells them about his travels across Europe, where he's an artist. Slowly the reader learns that her brother is a high school dropout who disappeared years ago. Once in a while he sends a scrawled postcard to Ashley, from whatever place the winds have blown him. What other secrets is Ashley hiding?

The author does a terrific job of pulling you in to Ashley's world. At first, I wondered why I should care about a girl like Ashley. After all, she does not treat everyone with kindness and she appears spoiled. But Kersher skillfully drew me in, slowly exposing the secrets of the family and Ashley's deep unhappiness. She will pull you in, too. I recommend this book to anyone who has ever known an Ashley.

1. What is the title of the book? _____

2. Who is the author? _____

3. What method does Shantay use in the introduction to grab the reader's interest? _____

4. Who is the main character? _____

5. What happens in the book? _____

6. Is the mood of the book? Is it funny, sad, scary? _____

7. What is the writer's opinion of the book? _____

Name: _____ **Date:** _____

As you know, a good paragraph has a main idea, often stated in a topic sentence, supported by details and examples that explain the main idea. The same is true of the paragraphs in a book report, which involves analyzing a book or story. The main idea of an analysis paragraph should be supported by details from the story. Here's an example, using the fairy tale "Cinderella." The main idea of the paragraph is underlined.

<u>The fairy tale "Cinderella" teaches children that goodness always defeats evil in the end</u>. For example, the two stepsisters mistreat Cinderella. They make fun of her and treat her as a slave. "Iron my gown, Cinderella!" one of them demands. "Curl my hair!" another orders. They even laugh at her when she wishes out loud that she could attend the ball. "You?" they exclaim. "Whatever can you be thinking of? How can you go to the ball? What would you wear—your tattered gray dress?" However, by the end of the story, the sisters are left with nothing, while Cinderella marries the prince. The main idea is Cinderella shows that goodness always defeats evil. The writer supports this idea by pointing out that Cinderella, who is good, wins the prince, while her evil stepsisters are left with nothing.

Directions: Think of a book, story, or fairytale you are familiar with. What lesson does it teach? Write a paragraph explaining what the story teaches. Support your main idea with details from the story.

Name: _____   **Date:** _____

Directions: Think of a book or story you have read. Write a short book report about it. In your book report, be sure to include the title, the author's name, an interesting introduction, some information about the book, and your opinion.

_____

_____

_____

_____

_____

_____

_____

_____

_____

_____

_____

_____

_____

_____

_____

_____

_____

_____

_____

_____

_____

_____

_____

_____

_____

_____

_____

_____

_____

_____

_____

_____

_____

_____

Name: _____   **Date:** _____

When you write a persuasive paragraph, you try to persuade the reader to do something or agree with your opinion. The first step is to state your goal, or what you want the reader to do. This should be done in the topic sentence of the paragraph. Next, you must persuade the reader to do it. This is done by giving strong reasons. Use facts and examples to support your reasons. Read this example of a persuasive paragraph.

A no-talk lunchroom policy would do more harm than good. For example, some students might be angry about not being able to talk. Also, students would constantly be breaking the rules.

The above writer offers several reasons why a no-talk policy would cause problems, but he or she has not explained the reasons with facts and examples. Adding details will help make the paragraph more persuasive.

Revised Paragraph

A no-talk lunchroom policy would do more harm than good. For example, some students might be angry about not being able to talk. If students are angry, they will probably not perform well in their classes. Also, students would constantly be breaking the rules. One of the hardest things about school is not being able to talk to friends during classes, but students have always known that they can "catch up" during lunch. The temptation talk would be too much for many students, no matter what the rules. The teachers on duty would then have to punish students, which could result in hard feelings, not to mention an overflowing detention hall.

Directions: For each topic sentence below, give one strong reason. Write one or more facts or examples for each reason.

Topic Sentence: Students should be required to wear school uniforms.

Reason: _____

Example or Fact: _____

Example or Fact: _____

Topic Sentence: The school lunch program could be improved by adding a salad bar.

Reason: _____

Example or Fact: _____

Example or Fact: _____

Name: _____ Date: _____

One thing to consider when writing a persuasive essay is who the intended audience will be. The way you would write for a classroom of six-year-olds should be quite different from the way you would write for your principal. The words, the phrases, and even the length of the sentences would be different. A persuasive paper will be most effective if it is written with the specific audience in mind.

Directions: Imagine that at your school the hallways are extremely noisy and crowded between classes. It bothers many students for it to be so loud. Choose one of the following persuasive paragraphs to write:

- a paragraph to your fellow seventh-graders, persuading them to be quieter in the hallways
- a paragraph to the school board, persuading the members to create a new rule about the noise in the hallways

Before writing the paragraph, answer the questions. As you write, choose words and phrases that are appropriate for your audience.

Who is my audience? _____

How well informed are they about the topic?
    uninformed   fairly informed   very informed

How interested are they likely to be in my subject?
    Not interested   fairly interested   very interested

Are they likely to resist what I have to say?   yes   no

What is my relationship to them?
    peer to peer   expert to novice   child to adult

My Paragraph:

_____
_____
_____
_____
_____
_____
_____
_____
_____
_____
_____
_____
_____

Name: _____   **Date:** _____

Point of view refers to the role the writer plays in the writing. Below are the three points of view that are most commonly used in formal writing.

- **First Person**—The narrator takes part in the action or has a presence in the writing. Among the pronouns the first person point of view uses are *I, me, my, myself, mine, we, us, our, ourselves.*
- **Second Person**—The narrator is addressing the reader. Among the pronouns the second person point of view uses are *you, your, yourself, yourselves.*
- **Third Person**—The narrator is removed from the action. Among the pronouns the third person point of view uses are *he, him, his, himself, she, her, hers, herself, it, its, itself, they, them, their, themselves.*

Many writers avoid the first-person point of view in formal writing. Their reasoning is that formal writing should be objective. In other words, it should be fair, allowing readers to form their own opinions about the topic. The first-person pronouns would be avoided because they sound "pushy." On the other hand, if you are writing for your peers about an issue that affects all of you, using pronouns such as "we" and "our" creates a sense of unity with your readers.

Directions: The following paragraph, adapted from page 121, is written from the third person point of view. Rewrite it in the first-person point of view. Then decide which you think works best for the topic.

A no-talk lunchroom policy would do more harm than good. For example, some students might be angry about not being able to talk. If students are angry, they will probably not perform well in their classes. Also, students would constantly be breaking the rules. Finally, some students might skip lunch altogether. These students might hide in a restroom or unused classroom just so they can talk to their friends.

_____

_____

_____

_____

_____

_____

_____

_____

_____

_____

The best point of view for this topic is _____.

Name: _____   **Date:** _____

WRITE A PERSUASIVE PARAGRAPH

Directions: Choose one of the goals below and write a persuasive paragraph. You can plan your reasons, facts, and examples on a separate sheet of paper. Remember to begin your paragraph with a strong introduction.

Choose one of the following:
- to persuade the school principal to hold (more/fewer) pep rallies
- to persuade the city council to build a skate park
- to persuade your classmates to keep the schoolyard clean

Name: _____   Date: _____

 Language Arts Skills & Strategies, Level 7 • Saddleback Publishing, Inc. ©2005 • 3 Watson, Irvine, CA 92618 • Phone (888) 735-2225 • www.sdlback.com

A research report gives facts and information about a topic. It is made up of several paragraphs. The opening paragraph states topic and main idea. The paragraphs that follow provide supporting details for the main idea. The report ends with a closing paragraph that wraps up the report.

The information you include in a research report comes from your own knowledge and from doing research—looking for information in encyclopedias, books, magazines, and other sources.

Making a chart can help you identify what research you need to do to write your report. On your chart, you should list what you know about your topic already and what you want to learn about it. You can also list possible sources for the information. Look at the chart Mia has started for her research report topic, **Gravity**.

What I Know	What I Want To Know	Possible Sources
Sir Isaac Newton played an important role in identifying the force of gravity	What research did he do?	a biography of Newton
Astronauts can jump very high on the moon.	Why is there less gravity on the moon?	a book on space travel
	~~In movies about outer space, how do they make it look like the actors are floating in space?~~	
Gravity affects the tides.	How does gravity make tides go in and out?	a science textbook

Notice that Mia crossed out a question that strays off her topic.

Directions: Fill in the chart with what you know and what you want to know about a person or profession you find interesting. List possible sources in the third column. After you write your questions, cross out any that stray off the topic.

Topic:		
What I Know	What I Want To Know	Possible Sources

Name: _____   **Date:** _____

A good way to plan your writing is to make an outline. An outline is made up of main ideas and the details and facts that support them. Making an outline can help you decide what information to include in your paper. It can also help you organize your information and arrange it in a logical order.

Write a Roman numeral (I, II, III, IV) next to each main topic. Write the subtopics underneath the main topic. The subtopics are facts and details that support the main idea. Start each subtopic with a capital letter. Details that support a subtopic start with a number.

> I. Scorpion—Description
>   A. 1/2 inch to 6 inches in length
>   B. Hard outer covering, not skin
>   C. Two sets of pinchers
>   1. One large pair for grasping prey
>   2. One small pair for tearing up food
>   D. Stinger on tail
>   1. Used to stun prey
>   2. Used as defense against enemies
> II. Member of the spider family, not an insect
>   A. Six pairs of appendages
>   1. Two pairs for grasping or killing
>   2. Four pairs of legs for walking
>   B. No antennae

Directions: Use the information in the box below to write an outline for a research report on manatees on a separate sheet of paper.

> — Manatees are aquatic animals. They live in warm, shallow water.
> — Their skin is gray and hairless.
> — They have a flat, thick tail.
> — Their front flippers are weak.
> — Fleshy lips with bristles.
> — They grow 7–12 feet long, and weigh about 500 pounds.
> — They spend their whole lives in the water like fish, but they are mammals.
> — They have live babies.
> — Mother manatees produce milk.

Name: _____   **Date:** _____

After you have completed the outline for your research report, you can begin writing the paragraphs. You will write one or two paragraphs for each main topic. State the main idea of each paragraph in an interesting topic sentence. Then write sentences about the facts and details you included as subtopics in your outline. These sentences should support the main idea of the paragraph. Use transitional words and phrases to show the connection between ideas and information in the paragraphs.

Directions: Write a paragraph for a research report from the outline below. Include a topic sentence. Use transitional words and phrases as needed.

I. Cocoa trees
   A. Grow best near equator
   B. Grows to 20 feet tall
   C. Produce cocoa pods
      1. Pods grow along branches and trunk
      2. 20–40 cocoa beans in each pod
      3. Each bean about 1 inch long
II. Drinking cocoa
   A. Enjoyed by Aztecs, Mayans, and Toltecs of Central and South America for centuries
   B. Discovered by Spanish explorers around 1500s
   C. Differences in taste
      1. Aztecs, Mayas, and Toltecs drank cocoa with red pepper and vanilla
      2. Europeans drank cocoa with coffee or with sugar

Name: _____ Date: _____

Narrative writing is writing that tells a story, true or fictional. A personal narrative is a true story you tell about something that happened to you. The story focuses on the main events, the details surrounding them, and how you and the other characters in your story feel and react to the events. Like any other kind of writing, a personal narrative requires planning. A chart like this one can help you plan. In one column, list the main events in your narrative. The events should be listed in order and should lead to a climax, or most interesting part of the story. In the second column, note details about each event. In the third column, make notes of others' and your reactions and feelings.

Event: Getting our first dog		
Event	Detail(s)	Feelings and Reactions
We saw a batch of puppies in the pet store window; my sister and I asked for one.	The puppies were black and white, fluffy.	My sister and I fell in love with them.
Parents told us "no."	They tried to explain why: expense, trouble, etc.	Disappointed, heartbroken
My sister and I studied dog-training books, tried to convince my parents	Parents said they would think about it.	Determined to convince our parents
Climax: One morning, we found a puppy in a basket in the kitchen.	It wagged and barked at us. My sister dropped her toast in surprise.	Never been so happy; "Nemo" was the best gift ever.
Nemo is now 2 years old.	Well-behaved, frisky, and playful	Feel as if I have a second best friend.

Directions: Choose an event in your life that made you particularly happy or particularly sad. Plan a narrative about it by filling in the chart below. Continue your chart on another sheet of paper if you need more room.

Event:		
Event	Detail(s)	Feelings and Reactions

Name: _____   **Date:** _____

Sensory words, exact nouns, descriptive adjectives and adverbs, and figurative language can all be used to paint a clear picture. They awaken the senses and make a sentence come alive. Read this pair of sentences.

The room was crowded, and everyone was eagerly looking at the goods for sale.

The room was swarming with people, everyone milling around the tables and pawing over the goods for sale like vultures around a carcass.

The first sentence states only the bare facts, and does not paint a vivid picture for the reader. The second sentence uses exact words that give the reader a clear picture.

Directions: For each sentence below, add one or two sentences to tell more about the scene. An example has been done for you.

> **EXAMPLE:** Maria dropped the box. <u>It struck the floor with a solid thud, followed by the clink and plink of tiny bits of broken glass.</u>

1. Max watched the fireworks. _____
   _____

2. Rachel smelled an odd smell. _____
   _____

3. Josh took a big swig of milk. _____
   _____

4. Dr. Dalton felt the dog's ribs. _____
   _____

5. Noah inspected his chapped lips in the mirror. _____
   _____

6. The airplane took off from the airport. _____
   _____

7. Monique chose royal blue velvet for her prom dress. _____
   _____

8. The cat smelled the open can of cat food. _____
   _____

9. Antonio listened to the rain. _____
   _____

10. Mrs. Costanza tasted the lemonade. _____
    _____

Name: _____   **Date:** _____

When you use dialogue, you use the exact words of the speaker. Using dialogue can make your narrative seem more real and "alive." Read the two narratives. Which one is more interesting and lively?

1. Amy and I were walking home from after long day at school. She was bubbly and chatty, and rattled on about this and that as we walked. Suddenly she asked me to carry her books for her. I glanced at the stack of books in my own arms, and asked her why.

Amy tossed her head and said it was because she was tired and wanted to be free. Without waiting for a reply, she thrust her books into my arms. Then off she went, skipping and dancing down the sidewalk ahead of me. I yelled after her that I was tired, too. She ignored me, and started singing a made-up song.

Needless to say, I didn't walk home with Amy much after that.

2. Amy and I were walking home from after long day at school. She was bubbly and chatty, and rattled on about this and that as we walked. Suddenly she said, "Anne, would you carry my books for me?"

I glanced at the stack of books in my own arms, and looked at her questioningly. "Why?"

Amy tossed her head and said, "Because I'm tired, and I want to be free!" Without waiting for a reply, she thrust her books into my arms. Then off she went, skipping and dancing down the sidewalk ahead of me. "Hey!" I yelled. "I'm tired, too, you know!"

She ignored me, and started singing a made-up song.

Needless to say, I didn't walk home with Amy much after that.

Directions: Write a short narrative about a time someone made you mad. Use dialogue to make it lively.

_____

_____

_____

_____

_____

_____

_____

_____

_____

_____

Name: _____   **Date:** _____

Directions: Write a personal narrative about something strange or funny that has happened to you. Use a chart like the one on page 128 to plan your narrative. Be sure to include details and dialogue to make the narrative lively and interesting.

Name: _____

Date: _____

In a how-to paper, the writer explains how to do something, such as how to make pizza or how to start a baseball card collection. The introduction of a how-to paper should grab readers' attention and then lead them to the main idea statement. The body of your how-to paper should explain the process step by step. Using transitions will help your readers follow the steps. Avoid using "then" over and over. Instead, strive for a variety of transitional devices. Your conclusion should make it clear to readers that the process is finished.

If a worldwide vote were taken on which country invented the best food, Italy would be the country and pizza would be the food. Luckily, you don't have to live in Italy to enjoy pizza. You can make it at home by following these easy steps. **Start** with a ready-made pizza crust or one that you make from a mix. If using a mix, follow the instructions on the box for preparing the crust. Usually, this involves blending a little water with the mix, allowing it to rise for a few minutes, and then spreading it out in a greased pizza pan. **Once your crust is ready to go**, spread a layer of pizza sauce on top. **Now comes the fun part:** adding your toppings. Almost anything can be delicious on a pizza. Try pepperoni, Canadian bacon, mushrooms, olives, onions, bell peppers—even pineapple or sauerkraut, if you're really daring! **Top it all off** with shredded cheese. Mozzarella is traditional, but almost any kind will do. Bake according to directions on the crust package. Once the pizza is done, grab a beverage and sit down and enjoy the most delectable dish known to humankind. Oh, and say a little "thank-you" to the Italians!

Directions: Write a paragraph explaining how to make a food you are familiar with. Follow the steps above. Include an interesting introduction and conclusion, and use a variety of transitional devices.

Name: _____   **Date:** _____

Some tests require you to write a short essay. They may ask a question or give a writing prompt. A prompt is a writing assignment on a test. Use these guidelines when preparing to write.

- Read the question or prompt carefully and underline key words that tell you what kind of answer to write, such as compare, explain, or summarize.
- Underline key words that identify the essay topic.
- Write a topic sentence that uses words from the question or prompt. Then support your topic sentence with details.
- Do not stray from the topic. Answer only what the question or prompt asks.

Directions: Read each prompt and underline the key words and phrases. Then answer the questions that follow.

Prompt #1

The local city council is considering passing an ordinance banning children from selling fundraiser items door-to-door. The council claims that the activity is too dangerous. What is your opinion of such a ban? Write a letter to the council, stating your opinion. Provide support for your opinion in the form of examples, reasons, etc. Attempt to convince the city council to agree with you.

   a. What is the topic of the assignment? _____

   b. What type of writing are you expected to do? _____

   c. Who is your audience? _____

Prompt #2

Imagine that you are cleaning your closet when you notice a small door in the woodwork. You get down on your hands and knees, open the door, and look inside. Write the story of your experience as if you were writing for a young child.

   a. What is the topic of the assignment? _____

   b. What type of writing are you expected to do? _____

   c. Who is your audience? _____

Prompt #3

Thomas Jefferson is considered the founder of public education. Jefferson's hope was that all children would receive a good education that would prepare them for the adult world. Write an editorial for the newspaper explaining how he might react to the public schools of today. Would he approve of them? Be sure to provide reasons to support your ideas.

   a. What is the topic of the assignment? _____

   b. What type of writing are you expected to do? _____

   c. Who is your audience? _____

Name: _____   **Date:** _____

A summary is a short version of a longer passage. When you summarize a movie for your friends, you condense it to the most important events in the plot. When you summarize a written work, you condense it to the author's most important ideas. You can leave out details that are not vital to understanding.

When you summarize, be sure to put the author's ideas in your own words. Summarizing a chapter is a good study method because it can help you better understand the text.

Directions: Read the passage below. Then reread it, answering questions 1–3 beneath the paragraph. Finally, write a summary of the passage.

Bombs Away, Beetle!

Perhaps no insect is more appropriately named than the bombardier beetle. Bombardier beetles belong to the ground beetle family (Carabidae), of which there are about 30,000 species in the world. Most ground beetles are carnivorous, hunting on the ground or in trees. Because many ground beetles are inept at flying, they have developed special defenses to guard against predators. But none is more amazing or effective than that of the bombardier beetle. When threatened, the bombardier uses a gland near its abdomen to mix together and heat two explosive chemicals, hydroquinone and hydrogen peroxide. It then shoots out a sizzle of spray—at the temperature of boiling water—right into the face of the predator. As if this weren't enough to discourage the enemy, the spray is accompanied by a loud "pop" as the chemicals explode! This amazing little creature is indeed one of nature's "hotshots"!

1. What is the topic of the passage? _____

2. What is the main idea of the paragraph? _____

3. Underline the key details the author uses to support the main idea.

My Summary

_____

_____

_____

_____

_____

_____

_____

_____

Name: _____   **Date:** _____

If you research a topic for a paper, you will be expected to provide a bibliography. A bibliography is an alphabetical list of sources you have used in your research. By including a bibliography, you are giving credit to the sources you derived information from. The following guidelines show the order that information must be given in a bibliographic entry. Study the examples to see how to punctuate the entries.

Books Author's name (first name last), the title of the book, the city where it was published, the name of the publisher, and the year of publication.

> Hovey, George. *The Pharaohs.* New York: Simon and Schuster, 1999.

Magazine articles Author's name, article title, magazine title, issue date, page numbers of the article.

> Bates, Judy. "Living Longer." *Time* 4 October 1987: 65-66.

Online magazine articles Author's name (if there is one), article title (use quotation marks), magazine or newspaper title, issue date, edition, pages or paragraphs, the electronic medium (such as "Online" or "CD-ROM"), the URL, and the date you looked at the article.

> "Carbs: Good or Bad?" *Maclean's* 28 February 2000: 110.
> Online http://info.maclean's.com. May 1, 2004.

Information from a website Author's or editor's name (if there is one), the part title, the source, location of source, the date of the material (write n.d. if there is no date), edition number, electronic medium, the URL, and the date you looked at the material.

> Harper, Emmanuel. "The Art of Quilting." *Sue's Sewing Corner* Centerville, IA n.d. Online. http://www.suesquilts.com/articles/art.html. 30 April 2005

Newspapers Author's name, article title, newspaper name, issue date, section name, page number of the article.

> Davis, David. "Welfare for the Rich." *The Des Moines Register* 23 January 2003, sec. News: D6.

Encyclopedia articles Author's name, title of article, title of encyclopedia, year of publication.

> "Animal Rights." <u>World Book Encyclopedia</u>. 1990 edition.

Directions: Choose three of the six types of sources above. Then, in your classroom or school library, find one example each of the three you have chosen. Write a bibliography entry for each. Include all necessary punctuation.

_____

_____

_____

_____

_____

_____

Name: _____   **Date:** _____

Proofreading your writing can make the difference between a poor grade and a good one. Here are some tips for effective proofreading.

Allow yourself some time between writing and proofreading. A day or two away from your writing will enable you to look at it with a fresh eye.

Before proofreading, reread your assignment. Then locate your main idea. Does it reflect the assignment? If so, read through the rest of the paper quickly. Do your details support your main idea well? There is no point in starting the proofreading process if any part of your paper does not answer the assignment. Revise and rewrite as necessary.

Assume the role of a reader rather than a writer. As you read through the paper, pretend you know nothing about the topic. This will help you see where there are gaps in understanding or where ideas should be joined by transitional devices.

Don't try to proofread for everything at once. You'll catch more errors if you start out looking for general problems, such as transitions and support, and then make separate passes for grammar, spelling, and punctuation errors.

Read the paper aloud, if possible, checking for general readability. Does your writing flow with a variety of sentence lengths and beginnings? How much trouble do you have reading the paper? Do you stumble over awkward wording or find certain sentences confusing? If you do, so will your readers. Put a mark next to any problem areas and go back to them later. Stopping to fix them will break your train of thought and make your proofreading less effective once you start again.

If you have a spell check program on your computer, use it. If not, have someone else look for spelling errors in your paper. A different set of eyes will see mistakes that you might miss. Afterwards, take the time to look up the correct spellings and correct the words yourself.

Check for subject/verb and pronoun/antecedent agreement. Locate the verbs in each of your sentences. Do they agree in number with their subjects? Now locate each pronoun and its antecedent. Do they agree in number?

Look for words you've left out or repeated. Add or delete as necessary.

Do not hurry the proofreading process. If you find yourself rushing through proofreading, try placing your pen or pencil on every word as you go. Or use a sheet of paper to cover all the lines below the one you are currently reading. A slow and thorough examination will give the best results.

Directions: Go back to something you've recently written—a paper for class, a journal entry, or a letter to a friend. Proofread your piece, following as many of the steps above as are appropriate.

Name: _____   **Date:** _____

PAGE 6

Sandhill Cranes, Cranes, Wisconsin, North America, Russia, Sandhill Cranes, Greater, Lesser, Canadian, Ontario, Michigan, British Columbia, Alaska, Siberia, Sandhills, Pennsylvania, Ohio, California, Oregon, Idaho, Utah, Florida, Texas, New Mexico, Arizona, California, Mexico, Sandhill Cranes
Answers will vary.
All answers should be capitalized.

PAGE 7

1. Civil War
2. Jazz Age
3. French Revolution
4. Jurassic Period
5. Olympics
6. Gold Rush
7. Middle Ages
8. Kentucky Derby
9. Boston Tea Party
10. Renaissance
11. Industrial Revolution
12. Chinese New Year
13. Mardi Gras
14. Earth Day
15. Super Bowl

PAGE 8

1. Republicans, Democrats
2. Spanish/English, Capital Books
3. Constitution
4. Junior High's, Leopards
5. Springdale Soccer Association
6. German, Lutheran Church
7. Greenpeace
8. Magna Carta, British
9. Southside Chess Club, Java Hut
10. Swiss, French, Italian, German

PAGE 9

1. OK, President
2. Dad, OK
3. OK, OK
4. Doctor, doctors
5. aunts, OK

PAGE 10

1. The Rise and Fall of the Roman Empire
2. "One Shoe, Two Feet"
3. "It's Easy to Remember"
4. "Hurricane Isabel Slams the Coast"
5. "The Princess and the Pea"
6. Miracle on 34th Street
7. The Chicago Daily Register
8. Romeo and Juliet
9. "Couple Marries 52 Years Later"
10. Malcolm in the Middle

PAGE 11

Union St., Scottsdale, AZ, August
Dear Sam
I'm, I'll, Your, Good
How, Molly, Is, And, Will, Also, I, With, Here's
Warmest
Aunt Rita
P.S.
Keep, It

PAGE 12

1. Ltd.
2. NPR
3. cm
4. CA
5. NHL
6. rpm
7. Capt.
8. NBC
9. PETA
10. gal.
11. Senior
12. miles per hour
13. minute or minimum
14. Arizona
15. route or right
16. New York Police Department
17. Company
18. knock-out
19. ounces
20. Colorado

PAGE 13

1. NOW
2. CBS
3. CD
4. NC
5. CPA
6. NASA
7. NCAA
8. USC
9. Pkwy.
10. WW II
11. MN
12. MO
13. CIA
14. IRA
15. Aug.
16. Fri.
17. UNICEF
18. VIP
19. USO
20. hp
21. BBC
22. CEO
23. ft

PAGE 14

1. French, Mrs. Dubonnet, United States
2. How, Jumpstart, Your, Exercise Routine, Dr. Lynnette Richards
3. Fenway Park, Boston, New York
4. The, Independence Day, Carterville Children's Chorus, America, Beautiful
5. Uncle Stan, Barbecue Shack
Hillcrest Drive, Frankfurt, Illinois, December
Dear Grandpa
Have, David, Chief Executive Officer, Public Broadcasting Corporation, Junior, So
With, Molly
Dr., IL, Dec., CEO, PBS

PAGE 15

? . . ! . ? .
. . . . .
? . . !
. . !

PAGE 16

1. Answers will vary.
Sample answers:
The class is going to an amusement park.
I love amusement parks!
When is the class trip?
Students must get permission from their parents.
2.–4. Answers will vary.

PAGE 17

1. elephant's
2. Mr. Sahu's
3. everyone's
4. Evans'
5. people's
6. Somebody's
7. deer's
8. committee's
9. politicians'
10. herd's
11. teacher's children's
12. jury's
13. correct as is
14. correct as is
15. correct as is

PAGE 18

weren't, can't, they're, they'll, they'll, that's, that'll, can't, she's, that's

PAGE 19

1. The plane tickets, my money, and my passport are in this bag.
2. Mr. Davidson showed Frankie, Vic, and I how to fix a flat.
3. The ball rolled off the table, across the floor, and out the door.
4. Would you like to play a game, watch a movie, or go for a walk?
5. My bulletin board is covered with photos of my friends, Lance Armstrong, and Prince William.
6. Red, blue, purple, and teal are the colors Quentin chose for his poster.
7. Brush your teeth after breakfast, after lunch, and before you go to bed.
8. Wear sunscreen, a wide-brimmed hat, and sunglasses at the beach.
9. This recipe calls for a pint of cream, half a cup of sugar, and two cups of sliced strawberries.
10. The pink slippers are decorated with sequins, ribbon, and silk flowers.

PAGE 20

1. Sometimes Rory stays up late, but he's always tired in the morning.
2. The procession of marchers carried candles, for the night was dark.
3. The computer is acting strangely, so let's take it to the repair shop.
4. Tracy tried on the red jeans, but they were too short for her.
5. Many people are afraid of spiders, yet most are harmless.
6. Use heavy tape to attach the sign to the pole, or it will fall off.
7. Lionel ran as fast as he could, but he missed the bus.
8. Sheri called me last night at 8:00, and I didn't get off the phone until 9:00!
9. Millie claims she wants to get more exercise, yet she always protests when I suggest we take the stairs instead of the elevator.
10. That band's last CD was terrible, and this new one isn't any better.

PAGE 21

1. The picnic starts at 2:00 this afternoon, Lindsey.
2. Unfortunately, it looks like it might rain.
3. The weather report, in fact, says there is a 75% chance of a storm.
4. The report could be wrong about that, of course.
5. However, they are usually correct about things like that.
Answers will vary.
Sample answers:
6. A little rain won't ruin our picnic, Louise.
7. Of course, we can take our raincoats and umbrellas.
8. My umbrella is big enough to share, I believe.
9. Luckily, the picnic tables are under a shelter.
10. We'll stay perfectly dry, as a result.

PAGE 22

1. Lianna, my best friend, moved away last year.

2. Carmen and Jeremy joined Rock the Vote, an organization of young voters.
3. Parker is taking lessons on the vibraphone, an instrument related to the xylophone.
4. The ring was set with a large cubic zirconia, an artificial diamond.
5. This sandwich comes with two kinds of cheese, cheddar and Monterey jack.
6. Today in art class we learned about Camille Claudel, a French sculptress.
7. Marcus's car, a convertible, is black with red flames painted on it.
8. It is easy to grow arugula, a salad green with a peppery bite.
9. Today's special, a club sandwich, comes with a cup of soup and a small salad.
10. Rachel asked Miss Chen, her favorite babysitter, to play a game with her.
Answers will vary.
Sample answers:
11. Jason and Sam went to lunch at Sandy's Subs, their favorite restaurant.
12. Sam ordered the Big Kahuna, a foot-long sub.
13. Jason, who had a large breakfast, could only eat half of his Heavy Hitter.
14. Later, the boys walked down West Avenue to the science museum, which had just opened.
15. Mr. Fallon, their science teacher, had suggested they see the new exhibit.

PAGE 23
1. Oh,
2. Ouch!
3. Aha!
4. Oh, no,
5. Hey,
Answers will vary.
Sample answers:
6. Wow,
7. Brr!
8. Oops!
9. Ah,
10. Grr,
11. Hurray!
12. Oh, no,
13. Phew,
14. Uh-oh,
15. Aha!

PAGE 24
1. "Who left their shoes on the stairs?" Toya asked.
2. Jennifer answered, "It wasn't me!"
3. "Maybe it was John," Michael said.
4. "He never puts anything away!" Jennifer exclaimed.
5. "Yeah, and he left his bike in the driveway yesterday," continued Michael.
6. "What a lazybones!" exclaimed Jennifer.
7. Michael observed, "These shoes are pink and red."
8. Toya asked, "Does John wear pink shoes?"
9. "I seriously doubt it," replied Michael.
10. "Oh, they're mine," Jennifer said sheepishly.

PAGE 25
1. "For your information," Hannah replied, "about an hour."
2. "I'm sorry," Amy said. "Are you mad at me?"
3. "How would you feel," Hannah snapped, "if I made you wait that long?"
4. "It really shows a lack of respect," continued Hannah. "Are my feelings not important to you?"
5. "You're right, Hannah," said Amy. "How can I make it up to you?"
Answers will vary.

PAGE 26
1. books:
2. subjects:
3. all:
4. decision:
5. supplies:
6. this:
7. clothing:
8. following:
9. McRoberts:
10. areas:

PAGE 27
1. he's afraid he'll miss out on midnight snacks
2. she prefers to be left alone most of the time
3. he runs on his wheel and climbs up a tiny ladder
4. Slinky would just love to eat him
5. she crawled under the sofa and hasn't been seen since
6. Saturday;

7. recommendations;
8. crust;
9. week;
10. Tuesday;

PAGE 28
1. sixty-seven, best-selling
2. half-baked, twenty-five
3. Great-Aunt, self-control
4. mild-mannered
5. fifty-five, father-in-law, snow-white

PAGE 29
1. jacket—
2. dogs—Reddy, Rufus, and Bear—
3. Incas—how they lived, what they believed, etc.—
4. cats—
5. sandwich—
Answers will vary.
Sample answers:
6. my favorite month
7. I'll get an A for sure.
8. I can't believe my friend Tom won't use one.
9. soft squeaky toys for dogs and cats
10. "I want to talk to the— the manager," stammered the customer.

PAGE 30
1. My uncle (the one who lives in Canada) is coming for a visit next week.
2. Payne Preston (is he a friend of yours?) invited me to his party.
3. The thieves got away with the money (about $10,000 in small bills).
4. My first day on my new computer, I sent an email to Paige (she's my cousin).
5. Mr. Mason used the story of Cinderella (poor girl strikes it rich by marrying a prince) to show that one's lot in life can change suddenly.
6. The steep Rocky Mountains (now paved with highways) prevented many pioneers from reaching the West.
7. Three of my four cousins have volunteered at the hospital (the fourth was too young to volunteer).
8. The storms (you'll be thrilled to hear this) will end tonight.

9. The car's paintjob (neon green and black) made people stop and stare.
10. What you really should do (although you probably won't agree) is find a new topic for your project.

PAGE 31
1. (so named for its call a clear [to-wheee])
2. [fizz-eek],
3. [1806–1868])
4. [thaw it in the microwave first])
5. [fah-sahd]
MRS. WHIGGINS [Looking puzzled]
I just can't understand what happened to my lovely pie. I set it right here to cool just an hour ago.
DODIE [Shaking head and looking serious]
That IS strange. [She glances down and quickly brushes crumbs off her shirt] Where could it have gone?

PAGE 32
1. immigrants / arrived
2. Most / were
3. none / were
4. men / wanted
5. They / wrote
6. They / described
7. matchmaker / would
8. She / would
9. groom / would
10. Most / approved
11. 1920, / 20,000 "picture brides" / came
12. brides / were
13. Others / were
14. husbands / had
15. husbands / were
16. brides / faced
17. They / faced
18. women / returned
19. most / stayed
20. They / worked

PAGE 33
1. boat
2. Max Wedgerman
3. letter
4. cat
5. recipe
6. towel
7. music
8. glove
9. dragonfly
10. piano
11. book
12. Jaycee
13. library
14. principal
15. shoes

Answers will vary.
Sample answers:
16. A mouse
17. Sue
18. The river
19. Alex
20. A replacement tire

PAGE 34
1. button
2. you
3. we
4. you
5. anyone
6. you
7. you
8. someone
9. you
10. you
11. Who broke the computer? I
12. Don't play with this equipment. You
13. Can someone fix it for you? someone
14. Put a lock on your door. You
15. Will that solve the problem? that

PAGE 35
1. has written
2. has found
3. has been living
4. will become
5. have been dancing
6. will be giving
7. exercise
8. burrowed
9. spends
10. will be
11. have lost
12. opened
13. was
14. lugged
15. had been running
Answers will vary.
Sample answers:
16. enjoyed the movie.
17. attracts visitors from around the state.
18. volunteer to help organize the triathlon.
19. is closed for maintenance.
20. rescued some kittens.

PAGE 36
Alexis, Aleesha, and Amber are triplets.
This morning, a humming-bird and a sphinx moth visited my petunias.
That desk and that gray cabinet should be moved into the den.
Seven boys and five girls signed up for the basketball camp.
Did Maggie, Patrick, and Tristan all have birthdays last week?

This evening, Carl and his family are coming over for dinner.
A nice bath or a shower would feel good right now.
Football, soccer, and golf are Thad's favorite sports.
The books, candles, greeting cards, and figurines on that table are on sale today.
Mario, Diana, Suzette, and I watched the lightning from the safety of the living room.
Answers will vary.
Sample answers:
1. Penny and Alexa
2. Andre or Latisha
3. gym class and music class
4. Carlos or Katrina
5. The walls and the ceiling

PAGE 37
The cat jumped out of Tamari's arms and ran out of the room.
Hector got goosebumps and his hair stood on end.
Either open the window or turn on that fan.
Victor has tried mountain climbing and bungee jumping.
Manny and Carrie will fold and put away the laundry.
Answers will vary.
Sample answers:
1. bought groceries and walked their dogs.
2. squealed and then would not start.
3. yapped and whined until their mother returned.
4. is flying to Boston or driving to Pittsburgh.
5. found the wallet and called the police.

PAGE 38
1. headache and back
2. yards and gardens
3. jacket and hat
4. this video or that show
5. green stripes, yellow dots, and bright orange horns.
6. the recipe, the parsley
7. me laugh
8. the broken glass, it
9. jokes, stories
10. a cactus, roses
Answers will vary.
Sample answers:
11. a song
12. her pet python
13. stories
14. drapes

15. the books
16. the state park
17. this movie
18. a speech
19. my computer
20. the sleigh

PAGE 39
Answers will vary.
Sample answers:
1. the gate
2. your sister
3. Shiangtai
4. her parents
5. his mother
6. the Ellis family
7. Dad
8. Francine
9. his friends
10. his teammate
11. d: stamp collection, i: us
12. d: game, i: children
13. d: secret
14. d: petals
15. d: fright, i: Helen and Rico
16. d: flavor, i: sauce
17. d: garden, i: visitors
18. d: projects
19. d: questions, i: brother
20. d: process

PAGE 40
1. concrete
2. abstract
3. abstract
4. concrete
5. concrete
6. concrete
7. concrete
8. abstract
9. concrete
10. abstract
11. concrete: Victor people, abstract: tolerance behavior
12. concrete: us boat shore, abstract: feeling sadness
13. concrete: Justine layer paint birdhouse she class
14. concrete: It piano, abstract: patience determination
15. concrete: George encyclopedia toe, abstract: cry pain

PAGE 41
1.–10. Answers will vary.
11. common
12. proper, collective
13. common
14. common, collective
15. proper

PAGE 42
1. selves
2. cherries
3. staffs or staves
4. messes
5. novels

6. wives
7. latches
8. roofs
9. Murphys
10. ashes
11. correct
12. monkeys
13. thieves
14. correct
15. correct
16. spies
17. leaves
18. batches
19. correct
20. correct
21. correct
22. correct, hooves also correct
23. Bradys
24. correct
25. halves

PAGE 43
1. sisters-in-law
2. volcanoes or volcanos
3. studios
4. sidewalks
5. Delgados
6. cellos
7. igloos
8. torpedoes
9. ice floes
10. truck drivers
11. Carusos
12. solos
13. altos
14. potatoes
15. passers-by
16. banjoes or banjos
17. zeroes or zeros
18. pianos
19. seventh-graders
20. echoes

PAGE 44
1. moose
2. tongs
3. homework
4. parentheses
5. advice
6. jeans
7. oats
8. pliers
9. sugar
10. lice
11. oxen
12. fish
13. wool, sheep
14. teeth
15. gold, silver

PAGE 45
1. car's
2. magazine's
3. houses'
4. Charles's
5. mice's
6. pliers'
7. men's
8. Tom's
9. evening's

10. dollar's
11. girl's
12. Mara's
13. neighbors'
14. teachers'
15. day's
16. actors'
17. Browns'
18. people's
19. fox's
20. moose's
21. the hotel's lobby
22. one month's effort
23. Anne's flashlight
24. the dog's health
25. Phyllis's responsibility
26. the opera singers' wigs
27. one hour's pay
28. the teens' skateboards
29. a lion's roar
30. Mr. Evans's car

PAGE 46
1. aunt and uncle's
2. Cheyenne, Gavin, and Melissa's
3. New York's and Maryland's
4. third grade and fourth grade's
5. highway's and interstate's
6. Louise and Emma's
7. Houston's and Dallas's
8. dog and cat's

PAGE 47
1. Zilker Park
2. players
3. Simon
4. Sylvie and Simon
5. children
6. It—the ball
7. it—the ball, they—the balls
8. They—the players, them—the balls
9. his—Simon's
10. their—players

PAGE 48
1. found their way
2. given its own
3. used their compasses
4. has seen her
5. donated their jerseys
6. stretched its long
7. have its shots
8. bring his guitar
9. lose his or her way
10. stowed their backpacks

PAGE 49
1. They
2. He
3. it
4. them
5. them
6. We
7. them
8. it
9. her
10. She
11. us
12. me
13. her
14. They
15. me

PAGE 50
1. I
2. he
3. me
4. we
5. me
6. she
7. them
8. us
9. him
10. them
11. I
12. her
13. him
14. her
15. they

PAGE 51
1. themselves
2. yourself
3. themselves
4. herself
5. himself
6. ourselves
7. yourselves
8. yourself
9. himself
10. herself
11. themselves
12. myself
13. himself
14. yourself
15. ourselves

PAGE 52
1. my
2. yours
3. Hers
4. Your
5. his
6. Yours
7. theirs
8. ours
9. its
10. Ours
11. its
12. hers
13. Yours
14. its
15. mine

PAGE 53
1. Everybody, singular
2. All, plural
3. Somebody, singular
4. Each, singular
5. Neither, singular
6. Many, plural
7. Most, plural
8. Few, plural
9. One, singular
10. Several, plural
11. does
12. knows
13. was
14. has
15. has

PAGE 54
1. these, brownies
2. those, bars
3. this, platter
4. that, recipe
5. this, potluck
6. This
7. These
8. That
9. Those
10. This
11. These
12. That
13. Those
14. This
15. This

PAGE 55
1. Which
2. Whose
3. Who
4. What
5. Whom
6. Who
7. Whom
8. Who's
9. Who
10. Whom
11. whose
12. Whom
13. Who
14. Who's
15. Whom

PAGE 56
L, A, A, L, A, A, A, A, L, A, L, A, A, A, A, A, A, L, A

PAGE 57
1. intransitive
2. intransitive
3. transitive
4. transitive
5. intransitive
6. intransitive
7. transitive
8. transitive
9. transitive
10. intransitive
11. transitive
12. transitive
13. transitive
14. intransitive
15. intransitive
16. transitive
17. transitive
18. transitive

PAGE 58
Main verbs: born, began, played, was, shooting, proud, was, won, played, was, participated, won, represented, making, breaking, chose, named, call, sum
Helping verbs: was, would be, had, had, had, had, was, has been, can

PAGE 59
1. celebrated
2. occurred
3. revolve
4. will enjoy
5. require
6. checked
7. will start
8. traveled
9. get
10. will zoom
Answers will vary.
Sample answers:
11. Marigolds grow very quickly.
12. I yawned during the movie.
13. I will accompany him to the show.
14. He confessed to stealing the car.
15. We oppose the new school rules.

PAGE 60
1. laced
2. purchased
3. snatched
4. skipped
5. revised
6. occupied
7. enjoyed
8. buckled
9. succeeded
10. married
11. The hummingbird sips …
12. The cat watched …
13. Xavier never varies …
14. The engine propelled …

PAGE 61
tells, sees, are, have, bargain, doesn't, are, steal, are, is

PAGE 62
1. man
2. pudding
3. plant
4. mold
5. car
6. One, needs
7. bushel, was
8. counselor, teaches
9. pages, are
10. One, has
11. students, are
12. mayor, attends
13. team, boards
14. apples, cost
15. swarm, eats

PAGE 63
1. did
2. put
3. blown
4. thrown
5. had
6. came
7. been
8. fought
9. threw
10. come
11. did
12. known
13. blew
14. had
15. drew

PAGE 64
1. torn
2. bought
3. held
4. wore
5. drunk
6. given
7. tore
8. broke
9. bought
10. rode
11. sold
12. ate
13. worn
14. held
15. sold

PAGE 65
1. future perfect
2. present perfect
3. past perfect
4. past perfect
5. present perfect
6. has
7. has
8. had
9. will have
10. has

PAGE 66
1. I have prepared
I had prepared
I will have prepared

2. we have gathered
   we had gathered
   we will have gathered
3. they have trapped
   they had trapped
   they will have trapped
4. it has enjoyed
   it had enjoyed
   it will have enjoyed
5. you have planted
   you had planted
   you will have planted
6. had decided
7. has dripped
8. will have stopped
9. has lifted
10. had disappeared

PAGE 67
1. active
2. passive
3. active
4. passive
5. passive
6. active
7. passive
8. active
9. passive
10. active
11. was scolded, [aunt], scolded
12. is surrounded, [pine trees], surround
13. will be covered, [floodwaters], will cover
14. are pleased, [improvement], pleases
15. were saddened, [news], saddened

PAGE 68
1. All the students saw the movie.
2. The parents will give a wonderful party.
3. The mean babysitter took away the children's toys.
4. Small children can understand this story.
5. The unknown runner shattered the track star's record.
6. The window was broken by the baseball.
7. The stories will be read by the author.
8. All the suspects will be interviewed by the police.
9. The scientist's lecture will be attended by fifty students.
10. Each contestant's project is reviewed by a panel of judges.

PAGE 69
1. sitting
2. setting
3. lie
4. lay
5. sitting
6. lay
7. rose
8. sat
9. rises
10. lain
11. raised
12. lie

PAGE 70
1. to eat pancakes
2. to put off decisions
3. to keep herself fit
4. to bury the nut in the hard clay ground
5. to fly commercial airliners
6. to take off
7. to learn more
8. to raise $100
9. to study engineering
10. to take him to the mall
Answers will vary.
Sample answers:
11. Canoeing
12. Skydiving
13. Reading
14. Knitting
15. Bungee-jumping
16. teaching
17. jogging
18. Orienteering
19. swimming
20. Cheating

PAGE 71
1. This → recipe, ripe → tomatoes, one → onion, Greek → olives
2. The → stores, this → mall, six → weeks
3. an interesting → discovery, wooden → crate
4. The hot → sand ← warm and soothing, Chris's → feet
5. Belgian → waffles, fresh → strawberries
6. The → library ← empty, this sunny → afternoon
7. The shiny → surface, the → table, the soft → candlelight
8. Many → people, a new → city
9. eight → years, my good → friend
10. two tiny → lights, the → darkness

PAGE 72
1. heavier, heaviest
2. newer, newest
3. more talented, most talented
4. duller, dullest
5. larger, largest
6. more incredible, most incredible
7. sadder, saddest
8. softer, softest
9. more helpful, most helpful
10. fancier, fanciest
11. warmer
12. oldest
13. hugest
14. cooler
15. taller

PAGE 73
1. more
2. little
3. least
4. much
5. bad
6. best
7. worse
8. better
9. better
10. better
11. good
12. less
13. Many
14. worst
15. more

PAGE 74
1. quickly
2. eagerly
3. always
4. never
5. extremely
6. suddenly → snapped
7. never → expected
8. extremely → loud
9. only → oldies
10. luckily → occurred
11. very → disappointed, unexpectedly → cancelled
12. impatiently → waited
13. barely → tall
14. really → hard, miserably → failed
15. seriously → damaged

PAGE 75
1. later, latest
2. more happily, most happily
3. faster, fastest
4. earlier, earliest
5. more carefully, most carefully
6. less, least
7. harder, hardest
8. farther, farthest
9. more nervously, most nervously
10. worse, worst
11. louder
12. less skillfully
13. worse
14. higher than
15. farther

PAGE 76
1. beautiful
2. quick
3. well
4. familiar
5. rough
6. well
7. really
8. good
9. badly
10. well
11. really
12. immediately
13. good
14. badly
15. real

PAGE 77
2. Campers will need to bring only one …
3. The speaker devoted nearly an entire …
4. That guy looks exactly like …
5. … I could easily understand …
6. I definitely heard …
7. … only I can be …
8. … of the only French Club.

PAGE 78
1. quickly
2. slow
3. Russian, the
4. good
5. really
6. extremely
7. smoother
8. farther
9. most distant
10. most
11. understanding
12.
13. peacefully
14. cooked
15.
16. fastest
17. fine
18. better
19. more forcefully
20. most experienced

PAGE 79
1. beneath the stars, surrounded by pine trees, beneath → stars, surrounded by → trees
2. in his locker, in → locker
3. according to this book, across the country, according to → book, across → country
4. around the house, behind them, around → house, behind → them
5. with cream cheese, around each one, with → cheese, around → one
Answers will vary.
Sample answers:
6. during winter.
7. behind the fence.
8. in front of the monument.
9. before you were born.
10. inside when the heat was off.

PAGE 80
1. have blue hats → uniforms, with puffy white plumes → hats
2. in the red shirt → girl, with blue stripes → shirt
3. of the castle → moat, was wide and deep → moat

ANSWER KEY

4. under the roof → nest, of the porch → roof
5. except Marcella and me → Everyone
6. from the program → actress, on TV → program
7. delicious → salad, with tomatoes → salad, from the farmers' market → tomatoes
8. for the stolen bus → search
9. new school → board, to the gym and track → improvements
10. of old jewelry → box, from her aunt → jewelry

PAGE 81
1. accidentally → left, her purse → left, at the party → left
2. sand castles → built, on the beach → built
3. toward Mount Rushmore → gazed
4. about her new baby brother → crazy
5. off his shirt → popped, in his soup → landed
6. the quiz results → go over, in the last period → go over
7. at the mess → look
8. around the yard → ran, madly at the birds → barking
9. for her hilarious imitations → famous
10. through the woods → leads, past the castle gates → leads

PAGE 82
1. beside
2. between
3. Among
4. besides
5. between
6. among
7. besides
8. between
9. besides
10. between
11. among
12. beside
13. between
14. beside
15. among

PAGE 83
1. The winners from Lana's class …
2. Somebody with muddy feet left …
3. … CD player with a bad speaker at a …
4. I saw on TV that …
5. … the show with my favorite actor on …
6. … bake sale at the mall to raise …
7. … new book by the author at the …
8. … open late on Monday and Thursday to …
9. … volunteers at the animal shelter after …
10. Every spring, the mother cat …

PAGE 84
Answers will vary.
Sample answers:
1. … bring any of …
2. … about anything," Liam …
3. … aren't any tickets …
4. … assign any home-work …
5. … can hardly keep …
6. … I never hear any-thing …
7. … hardly any people …
8. … was not tall enough …
9. … drink anything before …
10. Nobody ever wants …

PAGE 85
1. so
2. or
3. but
4. for
5. and
6. nor
7. yet
8. or
9. but
10. so

PAGE 86
1. tele, object to observe objects far away
2. ben, person who gives aid
3. vita, substance people need to be healthy
4. tele, object you use to talk to people far away
5. man, cosmetic treatment of fingernails
6. dyna, an explosive
7. vita, give something new life
8. vis, sense of sight
9. dyna, a family that has political power
10. vid, relating to television images
11. man, to arrange by hand
12. vita, necessary for life
13. vid, obvious
14. tele, a message sent along wires
15. dyna, very energetic

PAGES 87–88
Answers will vary.

PAGE 89
1. ~~Wee~~, we ~~lone~~, loan
2. ~~their~~, there ~~thrown~~, throne ~~rain~~, reign
3. ~~deer~~, dear ~~knot~~, not ~~no~~, know ~~won~~, one
4. ~~bare~~, bear ~~eight~~, ate ~~read~~, red
5. ~~waived~~, waved ~~past~~, passed ~~haul~~, hall
6. batter
7. bank
8. bound, bounded
9. firm
10. mean

PAGE 90
1. farther, than
2. fewer, than
3. affect
4. fewer
5. further, except
6. less
7. affect
8. accept
9. further
10. accept, then
11. except
12. than
13. farther
14. less
15. effect

PAGE 91
Answers will vary.
Sample answers:
1. slimy, negative slippery, neutral
2. cares, positive frets, negative
3. jeering, negative teasing, neutral
4. gruffly, positive firmly, neutral
5. reason, neutral excuse, negative
6. cold, negative calm, positive
7. challenged, positive attacked, negative
8. energetic, positive frenzied, negative
9. so-so, negative adequate, negative
10. lied, negative misspoke, neutral
Answers will vary.
Sample answers:
11. archaic
12. smell
13. cocky
14. plain
15. plagiarize

PAGE 92
1. B
2. E
3. D
4. A
5. F
6. H
7. G
8. I
9. J
10. C

PAGE 93
1. simile
2. metaphor
3. simile
4. metaphor
5. metaphor
6.–15. Answers will vary

PAGE 94
Answers will vary.
Sample answers:
1. gazing
2. regarded
3. stare
4. observe
5. lousy
6. spoiled
7. defective
8. reported
9. claimed
10. exclaimed

PAGE 95
Answers will vary.

PAGES 97
1. neroli
2. law
3. verb
4. Latin
5. on this page
6. four
7. two
8. around 1680

PAGE 98
1. Dependent
2. Dependent
3. Independent
4. Dependent
5. Independent
6. _wherever_ they go.
7. _even though_ she has a lot of homework to do.
8. _as though_ you could use a nap.
9. _If_ we don't get to the airport in ten minutes
10. _as soon as_ it got dark.
11. _unless_ you can think of something fun to do.
12. _whenever_ he wants.
13. _As soon as_ the lettuce sprouted
14. _so that_ it doesn't blow away.
15. _If_ I see Simon at the mall

PAGE 99
1. Simple
2. Compound
3. Compound-Complex
4. Compound
5. Simple
6. Simple
7. Compound-Complex
8. Complex
9. Complex
10. Compound
11. Compound
12. Simple
13. Complex
14. Complex

PAGE 100
Simple: 5, 8
Compound: 2, 3, 10
Complex: 1, 6, 7
Compound-Complex: 4, 9

PAGE 101

1. S	6. S
2. F	7. S
3. S	8. F
4. S	9. F
5. F	10. F

11.–15. Answers will vary.

PAGE 102

Answers will vary.
Sample answers:

1. A spoonerism is the switching of sounds in two words. One example is saying "bunch lox" instead of "lunch box."
2. William Archibald Spooner was born in London in 1844. He was a dean and president at Oxford University.
3. Spooner was a kind, well-liked man, but he was somewhat absent-minded.
4. His brain was so keen that his tongue often could not keep up with it. He frequently switched the beginning sounds of words.
5. For example, he scolded one student for "hissing my mystery lecture," and then added, "You have tasted the whole worm."
6. He made other mistakes. He once spoke of the "kinquering congs."
7. Sometimes he mixed up sounds at church. He once told the groom during a wedding, "Son, it is now kisstomary to cuss the bride."
8. He once found a woman sitting in his place at church. He said, "Pardon me, madam, I believe you're occupewing my pie."
9. He asked her, "Shall I sew you to another sheet?" She was probably laughing too hard to move.
10. Spooner died in 1930 at the age of 86, but his legacy lives on in the term "Spoonerism."

PAGE 103

Long ago, the king and queen of Troy received a message from the gods. <u>The queen was having a baby boy soon, the gods warned that the boy would one day cause the destruction of Troy. So when Paris was born. The king commanded that he be left on a hillside to die.</u> However, the baby didn't die. <u>He was found by a shepherd and his wife they raised him as their son.</u>

<u>A few years later, there was an important wedding party all the gods and goddesses, except the goddess Discord, were invited. Discord was angry. Because she hadn't been invited.</u> She thought of a way to disrupt the wedding party. <u>She made an apple with the words "To the Fairest Goddess" on it, she tossed it into the crowd at the party.</u> Each of the goddesses at the party was sure the apple was intended for her. <u>Hera, queen of the gods, argued. With her beautiful daughters Athena and Aphrodite.</u> Which one deserved the apple? <u>They argued bitterly, they could not agree.</u> Finally they asked King Zeus to decide. He refused to take sides. Instead, he sent a messenger to find a shepherd to make the decision. <u>The messenger returned with a shepherd it was Paris.</u> Nobody knew who he really was, though.

<u>Each goddess offered Paris a gift. If he would choose her. Hera offered him a powerful kingdom, Athena offered him military power.</u> Aphrodite, the goddess of love, offered him the most beautiful woman in the world, Queen Helen of Greece. <u>Paris could not resist that offer, he gave the apple to Aphrodite. With the protection of Aphrodite. Paris kidnapped Helen and took her to Troy.</u> Once there, he learned of his noble birth.

<u>Because Paris had stolen their queen. The leaders of Greece were angry.</u> They led their armies to Troy to rescue Helen. <u>Thus one of the most famous wars in all of history, the Trojan War, began. And the gods' prediction came true.</u>
Answers will vary.
Sample answers:

The queen was having a baby boy soon, but the gods warned that the boy would one day cause the destruction of Troy.

So when Paris was born, the king commanded that he be left on a hillside to die.

He was found by a shepherd and his wife. They raised him as their son.

A few years later, there was an important wedding party. All the gods and goddesses, except the goddess Discord, were invited.

Discord was angry because she hadn't been invited.

She made an apple with the words "To the Fairest Goddess" on it, and she tossed it into the crowd at the party.

Hera, queen of the gods, argued with her beautiful daughters, Athena and Aphrodite.

They argued bitterly, but they could not agree.

The messenger returned with a shepherd. It was Paris.

Each goddess offered Paris a gift if he would choose her.

Hera offered him a powerful kingdom, and Athena offered him military power.

Paris could not resist that offer, so he gave the apple to Athena.

With the protection of Aphrodite, Paris kidnapped Helen and took her to Troy. Because Paris had stolen their queen, the leaders of Greece were angry.

Thus one of the most famous wars in all of history, the Trojan War, began, and the gods' prediction came true.

PAGE 104

Answers will vary.
Sample answers:

1. After trying on the dress, Nina decided it looked better on the hanger.
2. Kanesha has a hard time studying at home because her siblings are noisy.
3. Eric goes for a run every morning before he has breakfast.
4. That director has made several movies, all of which were popular.
5. Every weekend, Mrs. Chen washes the clothes and her husband folds them.
6. The sign was faded, but we could still make out the words "Sam's Soda Shoppe."
7. Clay had trouble playing the song because he hadn't practiced it much.
8. Roger managed to find a seat in the crowded waiting room.
9. This building was the county jail before it was turned into a library.
10. The truck overturned on the sharp curve and hundreds of chickens escaped.

PAGE 105

Answers will vary.
Sample answers:

1. Gina had a toothache, so she went to the dentist.
2. The movie was about mountain climbing in Nepal.
3. Paulina visited Germany, Hungary, and Poland.
4. Because Euphemia sprained her ankle at practice, she won't be able to play Friday.
5. Sinbad yearned for the smell of the sea, the call of gulls, and, most of all, for the sight of sails billowing in the wind.
6. Reggie wrote the company a letter of complaint, but he never received a reply.
7. The old horse spent its days grazing in the meadow and basking in the warm sun, but it spent its nights sleeping in the snug stall in the barn.
8. Mr. Bartlett baked three pumpkin pies, a chocolate cake, and a batch of oatmeal cookies for the bake sale.
9. Jana didn't like watermelon, but she ate it anyway.
10. Olivia gave Pam a necklace and a beach towel.

PAGE 106

Answers will vary.
Sample answers:

1. Shamus entertained the children by using different voices for the characters in the story.
2. Lily kicked the ball, then ran as fast as she could to second base.

3. The heavy rains flooded the lowlands, swelling the riverbanks and causing a mudslide.
4. The council, the mayor, and finally the voters approved the plans.
5. The guard dog lowered its head, growled, bared its teeth, and attacked the intruder.
6. Italians, Hungarians, and people from Ireland arrived at Ellis Island.
7. Backgammon is a very old game which requires both skill and luck.
8. Diedre contacted the animal shelter, spoke to her neighbors, and searched everywhere for her dog.
9. Fish, crab and shrimp populations dwindled.
10. Although she was nervous, Alima sang flawlessly in front of 300 people.

PAGE 107
Answers will vary.
Sample answers:
1. Tran dropped his lunch tray on the floor.
2. Jorge fixed the broken cup with a special glue for ceramics.
3. The police tried to calm the unruly crowd.
4. Chris turned his nose up at the greasy French fries.
5. David tossed and turned on the lumpy mattress.
6. The expert seamstress made a dress from an old tablecloth.
7. The leaky faucet dripped incessantly.
8. Grandma took an old, dust-covered photo off the shelf.
9. Gary found the application form on top of the refrigerator.
10. Have you seen the new library on Colorado Street?

PAGE 108
Answers will vary.
Sample answers:
1. Iris made the appetizers, stuffed cherry tomatoes, and Jonah made the main course.
2. Jack's father, an expert electrician, put up track lights in the bedroom.
3. The hosts, the Jenkins, welcomed the guests.

4. Laura's mother served her favorite dish, lasagna, at the dinner to celebrate Laura's graduation.
5. At the museum, we saw a copy of the Mona Lisa, a famous painting by Leonardo da Vinci.
6. Alexis has a photo of The Bugs, her favorite band, in her locker.
7. Hannah, Amy's dog, enjoys lying in the sun and watching birds.
8. Humphrey Bogart, a famous tough-guy actor of the 30's and 40's, is often pictured wearing a trenchcoat and fedora.
9. The crown is set with sapphires, blue gemstones, and rubies.

PAGE 109
1. Tiring of the rain showers, the golfers …
2. Strumming her guitar lightly, the singer …
3. Strolling by the lake, we …
4. Disgusted with the poor service, the angry …
5. Working around the clock, the firefighters …
6. Frightened by the fireworks, the puppy …
7. Spilling soup the whole way, Henry …
8. Crying but unhurt, the child …
9. Embarrassed by the applause, the elderly …
10. Running as fast as she could, Eva …

PAGE 110
Answers will vary.

PAGE 111
1. Sandy is easily frightened./Things frighten Sandy easily.
2. The lights were left on by Lisa again./Lisa left the lights on again.
3. I lost your keys./Your keys were lost by me.
4. Hunters have hunted these beautiful creatures nearly to extinction./These beautiful creatures have been hunted nearly to extinction.
5. Workers completed the tower in 1753./The tower was completed in 1753.
6. I gave the pink purse to Abby.

7. Men's clothing can be found on the third floor by shoppers.
8. Employees must follow all safety rules
9. Morgan was stung by a bee.
10. The east coast has been hit by another hurricane.

PAGE 112
… I saw this light …
… It just looked like a red …
… It seemed to be coming …
… I walked across the lot …
… The sky was just glowing …
… Did you see anything …
… I noticed a flash …

PAGES 113–114
Answers will vary.

PAGE 115
Answers will vary.
Sample answers:
1. 5   5. 2
2. 1   6. 4
3. 6   7. 3
4. 7

PAGE 116
Life as a cowboy in the Old West was not as glamorous as movies make it out to be. Many cowboys owned only their saddles and the clothes on their backs; many did not even own a horse! Some had an extra set of clothes and a spare pair of boots. Most made between $25 and $50 a month and were expected to work long hard hours for their meager pay. On cattle drives, for example, cowboys were expected to ride in wind, rain, heat, and blizzards to tend the herd. If need be they stayed up all night chasing down strays and then spent next day pulling cattle out of the mud with teams of oxen. Sometimes, though, the weather was nice and the cattle drive went well.
Life back at the ranch was equally hard. If they were lucky enough to be kept on between drives, the cowboys had an endless list of chores to do. From sunup to sundown, they branded livestock, broke horses, mended fences, and planted and harvested crops. Modern cowboys might have sophisticated machines and tools to help with these sorts of chores. At the end of the day, the

cowboys retired to their bunkhouses, often just sod shacks. During the summer they lived with lice and fleas in their bedding, and in the winter, they scraped ice off the walls and huddled around a wood stove for heat. A wood stove is not the most efficient way to heat a room. Hollywood portrays cowboys as free spirits roaming the range at their leisure, but in reality they were overworked, underpaid, and miserable much of the time.

PAGE 117
Answers will vary.
Sample answers:
There
also
Later
The next day
Then
also
until late in the evening

PAGE 118
Answers will vary.
Sample answers:
1. The Smiles that Lie
2. Lianna Kersher
3. Vividly describes the main character
4. Ashley Simpson
5. the author exposes the secrets of the family and Ashley's deep unhappiness
6. mysterious and sad
7. terrific; she recommends it

PAGES 119–121
Answers will vary.

PAGE 122
Answers will vary.
Sample answers:
Fellow seventh-graders
   very informed
   very interested
   no
   peer to peer
School board
   uninformed
   fairly interested
   yes
   child to adult

PAGE 123
I believe that a no-talk lunchroom policy would do more harm than good. For example, I might be angry about not being able to talk. If I am angry, I probably will not perform well in my classes. Also, I would constantly be breaking the rules. Finally, I

might skip lunch altogether.
I might hide in a restroom
or unused classroom just
so I can talk to my friends.
Third Person

PAGES 124–125

Answers will vary.

PAGE 126

Answers will vary.
Sample answers:
I. Manatees—Description
   A. Their skin is gray and hairless
   B. They have a flat, thick tail
   C. Their front flippers are weak
   D. Fleshy lips with bristles
   E. Grow 7–12 ft long, weigh about 500 lb
   F. Live in water
II. Are mammals
   A. Have live babies
   B. Mothers produce milk

PAGES 127–132

Answers will vary.

PAGE 133

The <u>local city council</u> is considering passing an <u>ordinance banning children from selling fundraiser items door-to-door</u>. The council claims that the activity is <u>too dangerous</u>. What is your <u>opinion</u> of such a ban? <u>Write a letter</u> to the council, <u>stating your opinion</u>. <u>Provide support</u> for your opinion in the form of <u>examples, reasons</u>, etc. Attempt to <u>convince</u> the city council to agree with you.
   a. ordinance banning door-to-door sales
   b. persuasive
   c. the city council

<u>Imagine</u> that you are cleaning your closet when you notice <u>a small door</u> in the woodwork. You get down on your hands and knees, open the door, and <u>look inside</u>. Write the <u>story</u> of your experience as if you were <u>writing for a young child</u>.
   a. a short story
   b. fiction fantasy first-person narrative
   c. a child

<u>Thomas Jefferson</u> is considered the founder of public education. Jefferson's <u>hope</u> was that <u>all children</u> would <u>receive a good education that would prepare them the adult world</u>. <u>Write an editorial</u> for the <u>newspaper</u> explaining <u>how he might react</u> to the <u>public schools of today</u>. Would he approve of them? Be sure to provide reasons to <u>support your ideas</u>.
   a. whether Thomas Jefferson would approve of today's public schools
   b. editorial
   c. newspaper readers (mostly adults)

PAGE 134

1. bombardier beetles
2. it deserves its name because of its defensive mechanism
3. <u>When threatened, the bombardier uses a gland near its abdomen to mix together and heat two explosive chemicals, hydroquinone and hydrogen peroxide. It then shoots out a sizzle of spray—at the temperature of boiling water—right into the face of the predator. … the spray is accompanied by a loud "pop" as the chemicals explode!</u>
Answers will vary.

PAGES 135–136

Answers will vary.